THE CREATIVE GENE

How books, movies, and music inspired the creator
of *Death Stranding* and *Metal Gear Solid*

HIDEO KOJIMA

Translated by Nathan A Collins

VIZ MEDIA

SAN FRANCISCO

THE CREATIVE GENE

HIDEO KOJIMA

Translation — **Nathan A Collins**
Design — **Adam Grano**
Editor — **David Brothers**

SOUSAKUSURU IDENSHI: BOKU GA
AISHITA MEME TACHI by Hideo Kojima.
Copyright © Hideo Kojima 2013

All rights reserved. Original Japanese
paperback edition published in 2019 by
SHINCHOSHA Publishing Co., Ltd. English
edition published by arrangement with
SHINCHOSHA Publishing Co., Ltd.,
through Tuttle-Mori Agency, Inc., Tokyo

Printed in the U.S.A.

Published by VIZ Media, LLC
P.O. Box 77010
San Francisco, CA 94107

10 9 8 7 6 5 4 3 2 1
First printing, October 2021

viz.com

CONTENTS

INTRODUCTION
Memes Are What Connect Us

I began the original edition of this book with a quote: "A world without books is inconceivable."

More than six years later, my feelings haven't changed. But I, and my circumstances, have changed greatly.

Metal Gear Solid V: Ground Zeroes came out in March 2014, and *Metal Gear Solid V: The Phantom Pain* came out in September 2015. In December of that year, I went independent and established Kojima Productions. I had briefly considered stepping back from video game development to instead support myself by making small-scale films or writing, but my desire to respond to the wishes of my colleagues and fans quickly proved stronger, and so I chose to continue creating video games.

I rented a small office space—not even nine square meters—and began a fast-paced international search to secure staff and the software tools and engines we would need for production. As our company grew in size, we eventually needed a larger office, and I scoured Tokyo to find one. Meanwhile, we were simultaneously beginning production on our new game. There were never enough hours in the day to get everything done, but even then, there was one part of my daily routine I never neglected: going to a bookstore.

This is what I do:

I go to a bookstore, pick out books, take them in my hand, buy the ones that call to me, and lose myself reading them. Even on my business trips, I can't feel at ease unless I have several books in my bag. Picking out books and reading them is more than a habit I've maintained through life; it's a part of who I am.

I was a latchkey kid, and as the first one home, turning on the lights was my duty; opening a book in solitude was my routine. Books kept the feelings of isolation and loneliness from crushing me.

My father's early death contributed to a lack of role models in my life. But inside books, I was able to find adults and teachers to guide me along.

Books and movies provide only virtual experiences, but those experiences are valuable nonetheless. Of course, traveling somewhere yourself and taking in the local atmosphere would be superior. Climbing a mountain yourself would unquestionably provide a higher-quality experience than listening to someone else describe climbing one. But a person can only do so much, and so there is value in sharing in another's experiences vicariously through books or film.

Stories allow you to experience places you could never go—the past, the future, or distant worlds. You can become a different ethnicity or gender. Even when you're reading all by yourself, you're sharing those stories as they unfold before you with countless people whom you've never met.

We are alone, but we are connected.

That awareness has been my constant savior since my childhood.

And that's why, through this book, I hope to communicate the feeling of connectedness that other books have given me.

The intermediaries of those connections are memes, a concept introduced by the evolutionary biologist Richard Dawkins. Whereas genes are biological in nature, memes are units of information—

such as a cultural ideas, customs, and values—that are spread between people and passed on to future generations. I think stories could be fairly described as memes given form. As stories are passed from one generation to another, and as they are written and read, culture is carried forward.

Like genes are passed on through a connection between one person and another, memes are passed on through a connection between a person and a book or a film.

The world is filled with countless books, movies, and songs—so many that one person cannot possibly hope to experience them all. Consequently, I place tremendous significance upon the media I encounter within the limits of my lifetime.

Such encounters are acts of happenstance; they can seem like a product of fate. I have no idea what will connect with me, or where, or what kind of connection will form. And so, rather than wait in a passive haze, I desire to act with purpose and to cherish the encounters that result from my choices. I feel the same way about meeting people.

That is why I go to a bookstore every day.

I keep going so that I may create new encounters.

Every day, I come across all kinds of books, each offering their own unique connection: some catch my curiosity, some make their appeals to me, and some I simply pass by. Through the process of observing and recognizing those connections, I become better at finding encounters that are meaningful to me, and I further hone my sensibilities.

Not everything is a winner. That is true for books, movies, music, or any other man-made creative endeavor. In fact, nine in ten are misses. But among that other ten percent are incredible works of art. As someone who makes his living by creating, I'm always thinking that I want to continue producing works that make it into that ten percent.

This gives me all the more reason to train and refine my ability to sense the one winner in ten. That's not to suggest I'm doing anything special through this process: I go to a bookstore, I buy a book when I feel a connection with it, and I read it. If the book I choose is a miss, there is no reason to become discouraged. That is also part of the learning process that will guide me toward another winner. Time spent reading such a book is not wasted, but rather leads me to my next encounter.

Tucked inside nearly every book on my shelves is the receipt from when I purchased that book; I keep them so that I won't forget that time. Printed with the store's name and the time and date of purchase, the receipts rekindle memories of not only the contents of that book, but of the time I spent with it, from before I left for the bookstore, to the story's lingering presence after the last page was read; and of the places around me, like the bookstore, or where I read the book.

Whatever kind of book it was—even it was a boring one—the memory of the time we shared together is mine alone, and it forms a story uniquely mine.

Then, I go out to a bookstore again in search of my next encounter, and that one-in-ten winner.

If I visit the same bookstore every day, my route through the store will eventually settle into a routine. While browsing the store from a fixed route is more efficient, it diminishes the appeal and meaningfulness of going to the bookstore. Once my route becomes established, I stop seeing what lies beyond it. Going to a new or less familiar bookstore will disrupt my ossified patterns of thought, and though I feel lost, the experience can be fascinating. Even if the store carries the same books, those books may show a different side of themselves in a shop of a different scale, environment, or arrangement.

It's like how the same word can take on a different meaning depending on context or situation, or how you can discover a person's many different charms by seeing them within different social groupings. That's why—at the risk of repeating myself—I could never stop going to bookstores.

It may be less the case now than before we had the internet and social media, but bookstores still remain a repository of the most current information. One circuit through the aisles is all that you need to gain a good estimation of what is trending just about everywhere. Even today, a bookstore is a microcosm of the world.

Take, for example, NHK morning TV dramas. Even if you don't follow a particular show, a display of several related books could allow you to speculate that the show must have good ratings, while a cover-side-up stack of an actor's photo book will tell you that they are currently popular, whether or not you know who they are. A walk through the sports, how-to, finance/business, and manga sections will give you a bird's-eye view of much of the world.

Some will read the above and think, "Sure, but I can get that much from the internet." But that's not true. The information you see on the internet comes to you filtered and tailored to your personal likings and interests. In a bookstore, information of all types comes into your view passively as you browse, even on topics that you don't follow. Bookstores create a broader context that doesn't exist on the internet. Of course, for generations that have mastered it, I'm sure the internet offers its own contexts from which encounters will emerge. Denying that isn't my intention, but I personally choose to keep my focus on bookstores and books.

I want to bring my physical body to a store with books on display that I can reach out and touch. I want to walk through the aisles and notice a book on an endcap or a shelf, and then to take the book in my hand, bring it to the register, have the receipt put inside, and read it with total focus.

This insistence is not the product of an older generation's nostalgia; rather, the process of choosing a book or a movie has a certain universality that carries over to choosing people as well.

Discovering a one-in-ten winner from the overwhelming number of books in a bookstore requires constant training and practice. You can't just go up to the store, input "new release novel winner," and press SEARCH. You have limited time and clues with which to make a choice.

You can look at the front cover, read the sales copy and blurbs, read the summary and the afterword or other supplemental material, and skim the text inside. Then, based on those clues, you have to apply your own aesthetics and values to judge whether the book will be a winner.

The process is the same as evaluating a coworker, or their proposals, or various projects or plans. Those are no different than an unread book. You have to make the decision before you read.

In the case of a book, the penalty for a wrong decision may simply be boredom, but in business or other large-scale projects, poor judgment could result in a massive disaster that impacts a great number of people. Unlike visiting a foreign land inside a book, the decision of where to go on a real-life vacation could even be a matter of life and death.

This safety from harm might cause the imaginative experience of reading a book to be judged inferior to real experience. But that is not the case. Making contact with memes, in the forms of books or movies or other media, provides knowledge and wisdom necessary for going out into the real world; they are legitimate experiences all the same.

The way I go about choosing books naturally results in me learning about the real world.

I'm grateful that many critics consider my work to have originality and a distinctive creative vision. I can safely say that going to bookstores and picking out books is part of what makes that possible. By training my eye and my aesthetic perceptivity to find winners, I've formed my own viewpoint and values, which yield creative output with originality.

Finding books and movies through the opinions and recommendations of others is certainly important, but from the moment you open that first page, you must enter the world of that book with your own values and sensibilities.

There's absolutely nothing wrong with disliking a book that someone else recommended to you. Your judgment was made from your own point of view. If you liked a book simply because someone else praised it, that would be no different than retweeting a post on Twitter; nothing of you is there. Don't be concerned about being wrong or having a differing opinion. What wonderful results might arise when you discover a winner with your own eyes and mind? Something that is a winner for me may not be a winner for you, but that's all right.

I suspect the desire to communicate that idea might be why I develop video games, write essays, or contribute blurbs to movies or books.

The essays contained within this book are only a tiny fraction of the books and movies I've selected with my legs, my eyes, and my mind. This selection of works—rather, the broader context they represent—formed who I am, and therefore my own creations. The memes these stories communicated to me provided the energy I use to create, and to live.

None have diminished in their appeal in the years that have passed since the publishing of this book's original edition. Once more, I take this opportunity to deliver these memes to you, in the hope that they may form a bridge between us. ∎

PART ONE

MY LOVABLE MEMES

Originally published in *Da Vinci* magazine
between August 2010 and January 2013

STORIES OF THE UNKNOWN, COLLECTIVELY CALLED "OUR SF"

Inherit the Stars
Written by James P. Hogan

> *Our science fiction has come back to us. In the '70s and '80s, SF was not merely amusement, but also an alarm bell. It expressed our fears and our hopes. We have become too reliant on fantasies, and* Moon *offers us a reminder of the true pleasures of SF.* Moon *puts the charms of SF to good use, with lyrical explorations of philosophy and satire on current society. It's a perfect example of what I mean when I say "our science fiction."*

I wrote those thoughts upon *Moon*'s premiere in Spring 2010, and after being struck by a sort of déjà vu, I retrieved a novel from my library: James P. Hogan's *Inherit the Stars.*

I first awakened to reading in the fifth grade and immediately dove into mystery novels from all over the world. This continued through sixth grade; then, when I graduated elementary school, I moved on to science fiction, which was to be my partner until I went to college. During that period, I hardly remember consuming anything other than science fiction—and yet I never suffered from malnutrition.

I owe that to the breadth of the platter that was 1970s science fiction. Spread atop SF's dining table were all kinds of ingredients; a variety of cooking methods were being tested, and the cooks themselves were diverse. I tasted many, ranging from the big three (Asimov, Clarke, and Heinlein), to Vonnegut and Orwell, and all the way to Kobo Abe. They worked across an expansive variety of genres, and each created their own original dishes. These stories of the unknown could be broken down into many types: science fiction, fantasy, metafiction, and more—but collectively, they were all *our SF.*

But following the incredible popularity of *Star Wars*, at some point in the '80s, SF began to be pulled toward commercialism, and the genre left behind was a shell of its former self. The dishes and cooking methods were overrun by stale space operas and fantasies, and our SF had stalled out. Before I knew it, I'd completely stopped reading SF. Then, in a bookstore one day, I happened to notice *Inherit the Stars*. As I gingerly consumed its words, a nostalgic feeling came to me.

I had reunited with *our* SF.

Inherit the Stars is more than just a high-quality science fiction story with a positive outlook. At its heart, it's a completely new kind of puzzle mystery stemming from a question—*Why is a dead body here?*—that doesn't quite fit into a traditional whodunit, whydunit, or howdunit.

A corpse in a red spacesuit is discovered on the surface of the moon. Dr. Victor Hunt, a nuclear physicist, is presented with an image of the corpse along with the following explanation:

> *"That is the body. I'll answer some of the more obvious questions before you ask. First—no, we don't know who he is—or was—so we call him Charlie. Second—no, we don't know for sure what killed him. Third—no, we don't know where he came from."*
>
> *[...]*
>
> *"Let me say that from what little we do know so far, we can state one or two things with certainty. First, Charlie did not come from any of the bases established to date on Luna. Furthermore"—Caldwell's voice slowed to an ominous rumble—"he did*

not originate from any nation of the world as we know it today. In fact, it is by no means certain that he originated from this planet at all!"

[...]

"You see, gentlemen—Charlie died over fifty thousand years ago!"

How about that? I'm not sure if any other novel has so excellent a setup and as surprising a plot. *Inherit the Stars* surpasses the boundaries of hard SF. It's the story of teams of scientists who undertake a grand quest to break a 50,000-year-old alibi; of the catharsis of intellectual stimulation and puzzle-solving; of genre-bending surprises and feats. No mystery novel has a mystery as finely crafted.

Here is that sense of wonder we knew from our childhoods—our SF.

Sadly, Hogan himself joined the stars in July of 2010. *Inherit the Stars*, his debut novel, may go on being his most well-known work. But even more remarkable—much as the title states—is the new generation's ongoing inheritance of the memes of the once-dormant SF genre. This is not just a resuscitation of the SF of the past, but a new movement of young writers (including Project Itoh, Tow Ubukata, and others) who may very well have been influenced by Hogan himself.

The true nature of the "inheritance" debated throughout the novel is given over to us, the readers, to find. In fact, four other novels in the series provide more pieces to the puzzle. But the answer to Hogan's riddle isn't on the moon, or Jupiter, or Ganymede, or Pluto: it's within our generations—those who have inherited his memes. Those who are able to demonstrate that answer will become the inheritors of the stars, and only then will Hogan's Giants series reach the conclusion of the story it began more than thirty years ago.

■ JANUARY 2011

Inherit the Stars

Written by James P. Hogan and published by Del Ray in May 1977. Translated into Japanese by Hiroaki Ike and published by Sogen in May 1980.

A hard sci-fi tour de force, Inherit the Stars *is a masterpiece that incorporates the appeal of puzzle and courtroom mysteries.*

Teams of scientists are gathered together to explain how a corpse came to be on the surface of the moon. Their investigation begins with the puzzle of the dead body but leads the scientists on a search for knowledge that stretches back to the origins of mankind. *Inherit the Stars* offers the mental stimulation of science-heavy hard-SF and puzzle mysteries, combined with suspenseful twists reminiscent of a legal thriller. ∎

AS LONG AS THE FANS FERVENTLY WANT MORE, THE STORY CANNOT END

Darkness, Take My Hand
Written by Dennis Lehane

> *"I think there's a finite number in any series. You never hear people say: Oh, the fifteenth is the best. You never hear that. There's a point where a series has to end."*

In an interview given upon writing the fifth Kenzie & Gennaro novel, Dennis Lehane spoke about the series he'd fathered.

> *"I don't think I've reached that point, but I reached a point where [the Kenzie/Gennaro series] needed a break. [...] They are coming back, yes. Not this next book, but the book after that, I think."*
>
> – January Magazine, *March 2001*

The parental love in Lehane's words moved his fanatic fans to tears (myself included). Believing in what he told us, we waited intently (while reading his non-series books) for the day we would once again reunite with Patrick and Angela.

Ten years passed. Following the major successes of *Mystic River* and *Shutter Island*, which became international best sellers with movie adaptations, Lehane wrote a historical novel called *The*

Given Day, compiled a short story collection, and then, last year, published the sixth Kenzie & Gennaro novel, *Moonlight Mile*. But his new work betrayed his fans' expectations—this wasn't a revival of the series, but its conclusion.

After I turned the last page, I gave Patrick, Angela, and Bubba a heartfelt "Thank you!" and closed the book. But I didn't put it away. Not wanting to say goodbye, I retrieved the previous novels in the series and read them again in order—reversing time to deny parting with those characters.

> *"There's a point where a series has to end. [...] And I do think that the number is rapidly approaching: whatever that magic number is, where it's going to be time."*
> **"So people might be dying?"**
> *"No. Just riding off into the sunset or whatever."*

Lehane kept his promise. They did not die in the end. But neither did they go off into any sunset; his characters are still right where they were before, inside my heart.

This wasn't the only series to which I had to say goodbye last year. But I was not as shaken by the ending of Greg Rucka's Atticus Kodiak series, or with the passing of Robert B. Parker, creator of the long-running Spenser series. With Kenzie & Gennaro, the author and his characters are still alive, and I still hope I can meet them at least one more time. As long as the possibility remains, I want their story to continue. Such is the fan's mentality.

At any rate, I would like you to try reading this series and its stories of blood and violence in Boston's Dorchester neighborhood, of heartbreaking destinies amid hopelessness and pain; of drugs, alcoholism, robbery, murder, and domestic abuse run rampant amid the bottomless depths of poverty, where the only people who could be considered successful are gangsters or crooked cops. Even within a world with darkness and no future, Lehane's characters make the struggle to live. When you read Lehane's works of *literature*, I think you will see that this isn't simply a detective series, but an expression of storytelling at its very core.

Lehane has written six Kenzie & Gennaro novels: *A Drink Before the War*; *Darkness, Take My Hand*; *Sacred*; *Gone, Baby, Gone* (adapted into a movie directed by Ben Affleck); *Prayers for Rain*; and the most recent, *Moonlight Mile*. You don't have to read them all, and if I had to pick one to recommend, it would be the second: *Darkness, Take My Hand*. There may be no novel more powerfully hard-boiled than this one. A book of this caliber only comes maybe once in a decade—so superior that the first time I read *Darkness*, I looked into buying the rights to adapt it into a film myself. To be honest, none of the follow-up novels surpass *Darkness*. Between the characters, the plot, the foreshadowing, and the villains, *Darkness* exhausts the majority of the series' assets—to the point that I've wondered if maybe that was the real reason Lehane stopped writing them.

Metal Gear itself is a long-running series, arriving at its twenty-fifth anniversary next year (2012). Each time a new *Metal Gear* comes out, I declare to the press, "This will be the final *Metal Gear* I will ever make." My reason is the same as the one Lehane gave in that interview: all stories have an end. All creators, too, have an end. I would like to bring my story to its end before I arrive at mine.

So why then do I keep on continuing the same series? The answer lies within the Kenzie & Gennaro series. As long as the fans fervently want more, the story cannot end. A creator may try to end it, but he will never be able to turn his back on his fans. And yet creators and their series are not eternal. That's how we get stuck in this spiral.

I gave *Darkness, Take My Hand* another read, and there I found a message from Lehane. In his message, I found advice—and an expression of my own inner feelings.

"What, do you want to live forever?"

Darkness, Take My Hand

Written by Dennis Lehane and published by William Morrow in July 1996.
Translated into Japanese by Sanpei Kamata and published by Kadokawa in
April 2000.

A story of humanity struggling within deep darkness, Darkness, Take
My Hand *is the best entry in the Kenzie & Gennaro detective series.*

Patrick Kenzie and Angela Gennaro are a detective team born
and raised in the tempest of crime and violence that is Boston's
Dorchester neighborhood. This time, their client is a female psy-
chiatrist who is being threatened by the mob and who fears that
her son's life is in danger. The duo begins working to resolve the
case and unearths history and hatred long buried by the city and its
people. *Darkness, Take My Hand* is a hard-boiled novel filled with
overwhelming tension. ■

THE HEADSTRONG CAT JENNIE, WHO GREATLY INFLUENCED MY CREATIVE WORK

Jennie (or **The Abandoned**)
Written by Paul Gallico

I was in high school before I understood the difference between dogs and cats. I had never had either as a pet—not because I didn't want one, but because my mother had asthma.

Then, one special cat taught me the difference between cats and dogs: a tabby with slanted eyes and a white chest, from *Jennie*, a novel by Paul Gallico published in 1950. The Japanese translation was published by Shinchosha in 1979, the summer of my high school freshman year. I don't exactly know why I picked up this book when I wasn't a cat lover. Maybe the title reminded me of Jaime Sommers from *The Bionic Woman*.

The protagonist is Peter, an eight-year-old in London who adores cats but isn't allowed to have one because his nanny hates them. One day, Peter is struck by an automobile and wakes up as a white-furred cat. Suddenly thrust into the feline world and chased through hostile streets to the brink of starvation and despair, Peter is saved by a homely tabby named Jennie Baldrin. Jennie was betrayed by her human owners and abandoned to the hardscrabble existence of a stray cat. She teaches and trains Peter in all of the skills and techniques the former boy needs to live as a masterless cat: how to walk down the road, how to drink milk, how to hunt mice, how to win the favor of humans, how to stow away on a ship, how to twist his body in midair, how to groom and why, and the fighting techniques he needs to challenge the boss cat. While Peter seeks Jennie's help to go from a stranger to feline society to a 100 percent bona fide cat, the reader keeps turning the pages.

Paul Gallico's love for cats shows through his writing. While reading the book, the reader undergoes a transformation alongside Peter; the illusion is so powerful the reader will begin to believe *they* could talk to these stray cats. By the second half of the book, the reader has practically become a cat themselves and begins to hold special feelings for the character of Jennie, no matter that she's an animal. Jennie is prideful despite being neither beautiful nor perfect, but any reader, male or female, will have their heart stolen by her willful yet kind presence, just as mine was.

Everywhere you go, cats are the cat's pajamas. Bookstores will often have a special section featuring cat books. Mahokaru Numata's *Nekonari* and Heinlein's *The Door into Summer* seem to be mainstays. But the cat novel I keep on my bookshelf I never see in any bookstore. Recently, thirty-three years since the last time I read it, I took *Jennie* from the shelf and gave it another read. What I found surprised me: *Jennie* hadn't just influenced my view of women, but my creative work.

In *Metal Gear Solid 3*, The Boss confronts the player character, Snake (a stray dog), with a choice: "Will you live as a dog? Or will you live as a cat?" Subconsciously, I must have been inspired for her character by Jennie. The *Metal Gear Solid* series had been the story of patricide committed by mercenaries who belong to an organization (in other words, dogs of war). I created The Boss (a mother cat) to bring in the viewpoint of motherhood and stray cats. *MGS3* was born from *Jennie*'s meme.

Jennie is a lover, a teacher, a rival, a partner, and a confidante. The novel is much more than a moral story about a bittersweet first love and loss; it's a story, told from the feminine point of view, about the act of living, and it explores an intimate theme—how will I pass the baton (my "memes") to the next generation?

Just as every dream has an end, stories must have an ending. So, too, do Peter and Jennie part. Depending on how the reader interprets the meaning of this last scene, they will receive the meme in a different way:

> *Jennie was gone, the sweet companion of his adventures. [...] These things he saw and remembered for the last time before they faded away and vanished and in their stead left something that was neither memory nor dream nor fantasy, but only a wonderfully soothing sense of homecoming, well-being, and happiness.*

A very long time ago, I dreamed that I met a cat. When I awoke, I had returned to being a high school student, and the dream quickly passed from my memory. But as an adult, reading *Jennie* again, I realized that I had never forgotten the experience of that dream, not even for an instant. Now, as always, I carry *Jennie*'s meme inside myself. And so, when I declared at the beginning of this essay that I had never had a cat, I was wrong. I had Jennie.

■ **DECEMBER 2012**

Jennie (or *The Abandoned*)

Written by Paul Gallico and published by Alfred A. Knopf in 1950.
Translated into Japanese by Yasujiro Furusawa and published by Shinchosha in July 1979.

A story of those who live, told from the feminine perspective; told to me by a tabby named Jennie.

Paul Gallico's novel shares a surprising connection with me. The tabby, Jennie, is my *femme fatale*—not in the sense of a witchlike woman who brings fatal ruin to a man, but as a woman who, like Athena, goddess of artistry and wisdom, left a fateful impact on the *MGS* series. The adventure-fantasy of a young boy who becomes a cat will bestow upon the reader a newfound appreciation of the true substance of storytelling. ∎

WHEN WAS THE LAST TIME I WROTE A LETTER?

Kinshu: Autumn Brocade
Written by Teru Miyamoto and translated by Roger K. Thomas

A mailbox was recently installed in my neighborhood. Giving its silent figure a sidelong glance, I took out my iPhone, opened Twitter, and posted,

> *I pass a mailbox every morning and night, but I still haven't seen anyone drop a letter in. I haven't ever used that one, either. And yet every day, without rest, even in the rain or the wind, he goes on standing there with his analog mouth open. He persists even though he must be very hungry. The red mailbox looks resplendent.*
> *When was the last time I wrote a letter?*

Later, I was fishing through the contents of my home mailbox with a curious feeling. Bills—electric, gas, water, and Internet—a credit card statement, an ad for new cars from the dealer, the newspaper. That's all that was inside. Not even much unsolicited junk mail these days.

I tweeted,

> *When was the last time I received a letter?*

Actually, I tweeted that on the day this essay, the first for the My Lovable Memes series, was published in *Da Vinci* magazine. Some among my Twitter followers may have noticed the exact same message in both places. The pairing of the digital tweet and this analog magazine is just a little piece of mischief.

With the widespread adoption of cellular phones at the end of last century, our method for exchanging our respective understanding of things has been digitized on a dramatic scale. Text, emoji, and video have replaced our unplugged, natural voices. All communications, whether business, personal, or public, can now be carried out over text and email. Mutual communication is flourishing through personal blogs and social networks like Mixi, Facebook, MySpace, and Twitter.

But even in times like these, one love story hasn't lost its luster: *Kinshu: Autumn Brocade*, written by Teru Miyamoto in 1982, early in his career.

I love Teru Miyamoto. When I was seeking escape in fanciful translated books, his novels gave me the opportunity to come to terms with my real, true-to-life self. I read his novels exhaustively in my teenage years; *Kinshu* is my favorite, followed by *Haru no Yume* and *Ao ga Chiru*.

Kinshu is an epistolary novel made up of fourteen letters exchanged over a period of about ten months. The story begins in the autumn at a dahlia garden at Mount Zao, where a divorced man and woman run into each other for the first time in ten years while riding a cable car. The beautifully vibrant opening scene evokes the brocade of the novel's subtitle. The garden's autumn colors mingle with those of the worn and faded man and woman riding in the cable car to produce a landscape both solemn and grand. To a Japanese person whose preference for the color of autumn leaves remains unchallenged through all the seasons, the picturesque scene is bedazzling. Mozart's Thirty-Ninth Symphony also makes frequent appearances through the story. The imagery and sounds are remarkably vivid, especially for an epistolary novel.

After their chance reunion, the estranged couple begin a heart-to-heart correspondence, writing the things they hadn't been able to say before. Separated by distance and time, their letters are sometimes romantic, sometimes regretful, sometimes confessional, and sometimes scolding. Through their discrepancies and similarities, the past and present of the broken couple intertwine with the passing seasons like brocaded embroidery on woven fabric. By the novel's end, their futures are new and rich with color. *Kinshu* is a masterpiece—a beautiful, heartbreaking, and sophisticated story of lost love.

A letter can't go to multiple parties. It's not bidirectional. A gap will always occur between the time it's sent and the time it's received. The time and circumstances of its reading can't be designated, nor will they be shared by the sender and receiver. Once you let it go, you can't delete or edit it. Letters are a poor medium prone to misunderstandings and missed connections—which is precisely why I want to advocate for letters in these times. It is *because* a letter is a one-way street that the writer and reader are able to come together toward the middle. Through the exchange of letters, we naturally strengthen our ability to empathize and to understand our shared emotions.

And if we've forgotten that, *Kinshu* is here to remind us.

So take this opportunity to write a letter—to a relative whom you haven't called on the phone lately, to a good friend you haven't seen in a while, to a mentor with whom you only exchange holiday cards, to acquaintances you only contact through texting or social media. You don't have to send it. You don't need to stick on a stamp. You don't even need to show it to anyone. Try writing a letter to no one in particular. You might see something in it you forgot, and you might learn something unexpected about yourself.

Public phones have long vanished from our streets. It may only be a matter of time before mailboxes are the next to go. That red mailbox with the empty stomach in my neighborhood may die from starvation. But I hope that as people read novels like *Kinshu*, the red mailbox on my street will be reenlivened, vibrant once more, like a tree in autumn.

■ AUGUST 2010

Kinshu: Autumn Brocade

Written by Teru Miyamoto and published by Shinchosha in March 1982. Translated into English by Roger K. Thomas and published by New Directions in October 2005.

Letters—a poor medium prone to misunderstandings and misconnections.

Ten years after the dramatic collapse of Aki and Yasuaki's happy marriage, the estranged couple meet by chance on a mountainside ablaze with autumn leaves. They begin a correspondence, and as they both write about their unhealed wounds, they slowly begin to absolve their lonely souls. *Kinshu* is a beautiful love story only possible due to the one-way nature of the epistolary form. ■

THE DEFINITION OF FREEDOM DEPENDS ON THE POINT OF VIEW

The Woman in the Dunes
Written by Kobo Abe and translated by E. Dale Saunders

I n May of this year, a massive sinkhole appeared at an intersection in Guatemala City. Experts speculated that the sinkhole was likely caused by softening of the soil from broken sewer pipes combined with heavy rain from Tropical Storm Agatha, but the internet was in an uproar with people suggesting it might be a gate to hell.

Holes are gateways to other worlds. Their hollows conjure our feelings of awe and fear toward the unknown—and at the same time, even of base arousal.

The same is true of holes in stories. A character falling into a hole was utilized in *Alice's Adventures in Wonderland* and has been reused as a story framework countless times in tales worldwide since.

Kobo Abe is among the authors who influenced me the most. He excelled at unveiling contemporary society and human nature by way of science fiction and fable with the help of metaphor. His representative work, *The Woman in the Dunes*, uses the "falling into a hole" plot. The novel, a personal favorite, ranks among my top three Kobo Abe novels alongside *The Face of Another* and *The Box Man*.

A schoolteacher goes to the sand dunes to collect insects and becomes imprisoned in a house at the bottom of a deep pit in the sand, like an ant lion trap. A young widow lives in the house; the members of the nearby village have forced her, and the endless task of digging away the ever-falling sand in the pit, upon him. *The Woman in the Dunes* is a masterpiece that blends realism and eroticism. Though the novel gets categorized as literary fiction, I also recommend it as a horror or mystery story. Once you read *The Woman in the Dunes*, I'm sure you'll find that you've fallen into the pit trap of Abe's talent.

In a conversation with an American screenwriter, Ryu Murakami once said that all stories follow the same plot: the protagonist falls into a hole and either crawls out or dies within. When I heard that, it made sense to me; I could see nearly all stories fitting into that pattern. But in his genius, Abe would not settle for the ordinary. *The Woman in the Dunes* offers a third plot: the man finds a life inside the pit.

Even in *Alice's Adventures in Wonderland*, Alice's experiences inside the rabbit hole work toward bringing her back to reality. Not so in *The Woman in the Dunes*. When the man is stranded at the bottom of the pit, he at first struggles to escape, but in the end, he chooses to remain there. When he finally obtains his much-longed-for means of escape, he has an epiphany and comes to understand the freedom to be found in staying inside the hole—a freedom that he chooses while letting a different freedom go.

And that is what life is. Is that same third option not the framework that governs our society, our work, our families, our life, and our day-to-day life? Unknowingly, we all are lured into our pits, swallowed up, and we struggle to crawl out. But even if we make it out, nothing is changed. Outside, new holes are being dug; being trapped in a different pit is the only outcome.

There are many such pits in life. Some are made for us, and others we make particularly for ourselves. For every pit trap, there is also a shelter. To live is to fall into many pits. As long as you are walking forward, you will fall into a pit.

In that case, should we not try to find the best life in our current pit? Rather than accepting it as it is, or escaping it, or lashing out against it, try to find a new purpose there. There is freedom in leaving, freedom in not leaving, and freedom to be discovered in choosing to live there. The definition of freedom changes depending on your thinking and your point of view. *The Woman in the Dunes* taught me the meme that freedom does not flow like sand; freedom is the flow itself.

■ **SEPTEMBER 2010**

The Woman in the Dunes
Written by Kobo Abe and published by Shinchosha in June 1962; translated into English by E. Dale Saunders and published by Alfred A. Knopf in 1964.

Kobo Abe may have been using a pit as a metaphor for the norms that govern our lives as a society.

A schoolteacher who goes to the sand dunes to collect insects is encouraged by village elders to stay the night in a widow's home. The next morning, he finds himself a captive in the home at the bottom of an ant lion trap-like pit. He tries every method of escaping he can think of, but then....

Through documentary techniques and with plenty of suspense, Abe depicts a clear portrait of human nature. ■

A CHILD'S GROWTH IS ENTRUSTED TO A HARSHER SEASON THAT WILL SOON COME

Early Autumn
Written by Robert B. Parker

On a brutally hot day the calendar claimed was the beginning of fall, I went with my son, who has just about reached my height, to see the Yomiuri Giants battle the Hanshin Tigers. I drank beer and my son drank orange juice as we enjoyed our first baseball game in some time. My son, a Tigers fan, watched with excitement. I'm not interested in baseball, but during the lulls I'd ask and listen to my son talk about things that have been going on in his life. It's our version of a father-son game of catch.

When my son was still little, we went out together often. Baseball, movies, concerts, art museums, events. Swimming, skating, jogging, cycling, diving. We went on day trips, we went far away, inside the country or overseas; we always traveled together.

But once he started junior high, that suddenly ended.

He had grown up. He wanted to be with his friends from school and to see the world from his own perspective. By the time I realized it, I was surprised by how rarely we were playing our version of catch anymore.

My father passed away when I was thirteen. I have no memory of going through adolescence with a dad. *How do I approach my son in the spring of his adulthood? How close or distant should I be? I don't have the slightest clue.* As I was wrestling with that internal dilemma, I pulled a favorite book from my shelves and flipped through the pages. It was *Early Autumn*, a Spenser detective novel. The long-running series was created by novelist Robert B. Parker, who died suddenly in January 2010 at seventy-seven. Spenser is popular all over the world.

As a graduate student, Parker studied Raymond Chandler, and through his Spenser series, he is widely considered to be the successor of writers of hard-boiled fiction like Chandler and Macdonald. But his novels aren't "man books," infatuated with Hemingway-like machismo. Parker offers lean and simple prose; extensive knowledge of fashion, cooking, and sports; cool, witty dialogue; and a snappy, charming cast of regulars, like Spenser's lover Susan and his ally Hawk. And while being hardboiled, the Spenser novels display a literary craft only Parker could produce.

Early Autumn was his seventh Spenser novel, and one of his standouts, loved not only by fans of hard-boiled fiction but readers in general for its poignant story of fatherhood.

Paul is a fifteen-year-old boy who is neglected by his parents. When he goes missing, his mother hires Spenser to find and return him. The detective learns the boy's father had kidnapped him. As Spenser comes closer to the truth, he chooses to rescue the boy from both his parents rather than pursue a more legal solution. Having received no guidance in life, Paul is withdrawn and must be made self-reliant, and Spenser devotes himself toward hammering into Paul the ability to live as his own person. Through their cohabitation, Paul gradually opens himself up and finds a purpose.

Their conversation at the novel's conclusion is stunningly beautiful:

> *"You'll have to catch up. But you can. Look at what you did in one summer."*
>
> *"Except I wasn't catching up on anything," Paul said.*
> *"Yeah, you were."*

"What?"
"Life."

Over the summer, Paul had spread out his leaves, and his face was tanned and full of life.

And *Early Autumn* ends with this:

"Let's go in and eat," I said.
"Okay."
"Winter's coming."

Paul's continued growth is entrusted to a harsher season that will soon come.

I'm not Spenser. I can't teach my children carpentry, boxing, and cooking. I can't expose them to scenes of violence. Like Spenser says, you can only teach the things you can do yourself, and of the world you've seen yourself, and in your own way. But the game of catch that is teaching and learning will broaden your future; the pitches of confidence you throw to your children over a season will someday connect them to their destiny. To be autonomous is to walk forward with a purpose.

Our baseball game ended at Giants 9, Tigers 1. We headed home from the Tokyo Dome, my son silent in the wake of his team's loss. This time I talked about how things were going in my life. Until we got home, I showered him with all the stories that I'd let build up, and this too became another valuable game of catch.

Then, in the harsh, lingering heat of early autumn, I played ball with my second son (who had just turned four) in a park for the first time. This was another season. In one long summer, I found the beginning of two seasons.

■ NOVEMBER 2010

Early Autumn

Written by Robert B. Parker and published by Delacorte Press in 1981. Translated into Japanese by Mitsu Kikuchi and published by Hayakawa in September 1982.

Spenser coaches a boy in how to live. Their conversation in the last chapter is stunningly beautiful.

At the age of fifteen, Paul has been taught nothing of life by his self-interested, neglectful parents. He is emotionally withdrawn and shows no interest in anything at all. Tough-as-nails private detective Spenser spends a summer by a lake with the boy and trains him to become an autonomous, self-reliant man. *Early Autumn* is a hard-boiled detective novel depicting a boy's rapid maturation, and a masterwork that shows the importance of fathers (and all adults) teaching the next generation. ■

AND THEN THE KOJIMA WHO HATED BOOKS WAS GONE

And Then There Were None
Written by Agatha Christie

Were you a reader from a young age?
No, I didn't like reading when I was a small child.

> *Ten little Soldier Boys went out to dine;*
> *One choked his little self and then there were nine.*

When did you start reading?
When I was in fifth grade. Before then I didn't read; I disliked reading without ever having tried it.

> *Nine little Soldier Boys sat up very late;*
> *One overslept himself and then there were eight.*

You must have come across some very interesting books, then.
I was reading nothing but mystery novels, and they kept me up late.

> *Eight little Soldier Boys travelling in Devon;*
> *One said he'd stay there and then there were seven.*

Mystery novels? Japanese ones?
No, I was exclusively reading Agatha Christie.

Seven little Soldier Boys chopping up sticks;
One chopped himself in half and then there were six.

What was the first book to make you realize that you liked to read?
The one that lit a fire under my curiosity was *Murder on the Orient Express*.

Six little Soldier Boys playing with a hive;
A bumblebee stung one and then there were five.

What made you decide to read that book?
It was made into a movie. I just wanted to see what the book was like, without really intending on reading it, but the novel struck deep.

Five little Soldier Boys going in for law;
One got in Chancery and then there were four.

And then you were hooked?
By the time I got to junior high, I think I had read every Christie I could get my hands on.

Four little Soldier Boys going out to sea;
A red herring swallowed one and then there were three.

Why did Christie take such a hold over you when you hadn't been a reader before?
Well...I don't really remember.

Three little Soldier Boys walking in the zoo;
A big bear hugged one and then there were two.

Wasn't 2010 the 120ᵗʰ anniversary of Christie's birth?
It was. I saw a display when I was in the bookstore. And now Christie has hooked me again. I'm currently rereading her novels.

Two little Soldier Boys sitting in the sun;
One got frizzled up and then there was one.

And did you solve the mystery? Have you learned what made you so passionate about her books?
Yeah, that fire rekindled as I read her most significant novels.

One little Soldier Boy left all alone;
He went out and hanged himself and then there were none.

Is there one you'd recommend to someone who hasn't read Christie before?
Hmm...well, the ending of *The Murder of Roger Ackroyd* is shocking enough to take your breath away, so maybe...

What if you could only leave one behind?
All right, I'll take a firm position. That would be *And Then There Were None*.

A locked-room mystery wherein everyone dies shouldn't work. What's amazing about this groundbreaking premise is that the misdirections and the trick ending can still surprise today's reader and make them think, "So that's how she did it!"

In any case, Christie is easy to read. Hers are not the kind of novels you read closely, but rather in a casual way, like how you'd approach a quiz show or video game. Her books are a perfect length and density. Though her stories contain a greater-than-typical number of characters, the characters are not complex and are quickly familiarized. And, most importantly, even though her stories deal with murder, they aren't depressing. That's not to suggest that Christie doesn't provide motives proper for killing. But whatever grudge or hatred motivates the crime, it isn't the kind that stays with you after the book is done. Unlike modern mysteries, they don't place an emphasis on social issues. They are intellectual games that focus on dilemma and deceit. And much like action or puzzle games, the more you read them, the better you get at it. You'll gradually learn her patterns and will become able to get ahead of her—and then you can test your skills on the next book. That said, if you get sloppy, Christie will trounce you. As you test your intellect against Christie's, you'll develop "gray cells" surpassing Poirot's, and you'll become a lover of books of all kinds.

That does sound interesting. So, who killed the ten people?
Eleven people.

What? Weren't there ten people brought together?
No, there were eleven in total.

I don't think that's right. I'm sure only ten bodies were found.
After "there were none," one more person was killed.

Who?
The reader.

The what?
At the end, Christie's charms left another victim. Me.

Aha. And then the Kojima who hated books was gone.

■ FEBRUARY 2011

And Then There Were None

Written by Agatha Christie and published in twenty-three parts in the
Daily Express beginning in June, 1939, then published as a novel by
Collins Crime Club in the same year. Translated into Japanese by Shunji
Shimizu and serialized in *Star* magazine in 1939, then published as a novel
by Hayakawa in 1955. A new translation by Hisae Aoki was published
in 2007.

A remarkably crafty locked-room multiple-murder mystery...
with no killer?

Ten people are gathered on an isolated island. Their host is nowhere
to be found, and a mysterious voice exposes their past crimes. Then
they begin to be killed off in accordance to a children's nursery
rhyme. *And Then There Were None* is an important classic among the
locked-room mystery genre, with an inventive structure and depictions of character. For this occasion, I read a new edition published
in the fall of 2010 for Christie's 120th anniversary. ■

WHAT LI ZHENG EXPRESSED AS "TIMID PRIDE" AND "DISDAINFUL SHYNESS" OVERLAPS WITH WHO I ONCE WAS

"The Moon over the Mountain"
Written by Atsushi Nakajima and translated by Paul McCarthy

I became a tiger.
Not a tiger like the masked hero in the famous anime, *Tiger Mask*. ("Tiger! Tiger! Be the tiger!")
When I returned to my tiger state, I became the man-eating tiger from "The Moon over the Mountain."

"If my fur looks wet, it is not only with the night dew..."

The sublime indirectness of that line struck me so hard when I first read it that I questioned my life up until that point. Even to this day, you can find Atsushi Nakajima's "The Moon over the Mountain" in high school textbooks all across Japan.
I was in high school, ignorant of the world, and oh so proud of myself for only reading foreign science fiction and mysteries. When

I came in contact with that sentence in contemporary Japanese literature class, I was dumbstruck.

Should a line that beautiful even be able to exist? It wasn't that I was jealous; the beauty exuded by the Japanese phrase gave me chills. Upon reading the short story, I took every opportunity—whether in the classroom, at home, or wherever—to read it again and again aloud, to the point that I memorized the story in its entirety.

For many years, I proudly assumed that certainly no one else in the world would have memorized "The Moon over the Mountain" from start to finish. Later I learned—from an interview or something—that Koji Yanagi, a popular author who wrote an adaptation/continuation of the same short story (called "The Moon and the Tiger") had also memorized it during his school days.

"The Moon over the Mountain" is Atsushi Nakajima's adaptation of a classic Chinese tale written by Li Jingliang.

Reading this story aloud in Japanese reveals the exceptional qualities of its sound and rhythm. Kanji is at its essence a logographic writing system. It is said that when a reader's mind is parsing kanji, the processing is handled by the visually oriented right side of the brain, and so reading "The Moon over the Mountain" stimulates the same parts of the brain as the distinctively Japanese media of manga and *gekiga*. Even though the story is only in text, the use of kanji functions the same as adding picture or sound; the writing can be digested with both sides of the brain working in balance. The conversion of the tale from *kanbun* (a form of classical Chinese once used in Japan), the writing's harmony with the Japanese language, and Atsushi Nakajima's exceptional eye for adaptation all combine to lift "The Moon over the Mountain" to beautiful heights. When I was a boy posing as a writer, whose style imitated the translated fiction I read, "The Moon over the Mountain" absolutely floored me.

I was in junior high when I began writing stories in earnest. It started when my teacher copied a well-known *kanbun* text onto the blackboard and told us:

"Convert this from *kanbun* into modern Japanese, and expand it and make it into a story."

I bit into those few lines of *kanbun*, digested them, supplemented them, and significantly reinterpreted them into roughly ten pages. My teacher took special notice of my work and gave my story high praise in front of the class. Before then, I'd been more documenting stories, with a movie plot–like approach, rather than writing them, but now I began to purposefully write real narratives. Looking back, that assignment followed the same process Atsushi Nakajima used to create "The Moon over the Mountain."

Later, I found another deep connection to "The Moon over the Mountain."

After I encountered "The Moon over the Mountain," I continued to write stories. I didn't have a mentor, and I looked down upon my classmates who were at the mercy of school entrance exams. I steadily nurtured my sense of superiority and kept to myself as I wrote stories that would never be published.

> *I hoped to make a name for myself as a poet, but I never attached myself to a teacher or sought out the company of other poets who might have helped me to improve my skill. At the same time, I had no intention of ranking myself together with the common, unpoetic herd. But this was the result of my timid pride and a disdainful shyness.*

At first, I would submit my writings to various literary competitions, and my dream was big—to publish my own work. But when I went to senior high, I kept writing stories but stopped submitting them anywhere. I believe that the cause overlapped with what the poet-turned-tiger Li Zheng, the main character of the story, expressed as "timid pride" and "disdainful shyness."

> *I realize now that I wasted what little real talent I had. [...] [A]ll there was in me was a cowardly fear that my lack of talent*

might be revealed and a lazy hatred for taking the pains needed to nurture it. There are very many men with talent far weaker than mine who have become splendid poets because they devoted themselves to polishing and improving what they had.

Without knowing it, I had become a tiger—and a game designer is my tiger form.

No, whether the poems are good or bad, I would not rest easy in my grave without passing these poems on to later generations, since they represent my deepest passion in life, even to the point of losing my fortune and my sanity.

Like that poet, I too have regressed into a tiger form, but when it comes to the meaning of the howl at the story's end, Li Zheng and I are very different. In my case, the moment I became a tiger, I shed my pride and shyness completely.

By becoming the tiger, I found a different way to pass on my stories than the one I had so rigidly insisted upon. And so, even as a tiger, I intend to keep on howling into the later generations. Those stories will become new memes, not as prose, but as video games.

■ APRIL 2011

"The Moon over the Mountain"

Written by Atsushi Nakajima and published by Bungakukai magazine in 1942. Translated into English by Paul McCarthy and published by Autumn Hill Books in 2011 as part of the collection *The Moon over the Mountain and Other Stories.*

A refined, emotionally evocative, and elegantly told depiction of human sadness and longing.

The Moon over the Mountain and Other Stories collects several short stories with vivid explorations of the nature of humanity written by an early–Showa era master who died at the young age of thirty-three. "The Moon Over the Mountain" was a major influence for me. The prose is honed down to the very minimum and races down the page, and reading it aloud produces a pleasing rhythm and melancholic melody. The writing is so exquisite I can't help but gasp. ∎

.

FOR ME, THE HANKYU RAILWAY IS A TIME MACHINE CONNECTING MY MEMORIES TO MY HOMETOWN

Hankyu Densha (Hankyu Railway)
Written by Hiro Arikawa

Hankyu is a private railway network in the Kansai region. Its distinctive maroon-painted cars and retro interiors are highly popular not only with train enthusiasts, but also with younger women who consider the aesthetic "cute." Stand on the train platform and you'll hear female tourists (and many others) saying with surprise, "Wow, cool!"

If someone were to ask me what I think of when I picture a train, it would be those maroon carriages—the classic Hankyu train running through the mountain valleys of Kansai. I was born in Soshigaya, where an Odakyu line runs, and then I lived in Tsujido, along the JR Tokaido Line, until I was three. Having moved to the Kansai region so young, I have practically no memories of the Odakyu or any other trains in Tokyo.

Our family relocated to Ibaraki city, far from Tokyo, for my father's job. Ibaraki has a stop on the JR line (back then it was the public Japanese National Rail), but our house was closer to the Hankyu Ibaraki-shi Station, so that was the one we used every time we went to Kyoto or Osaka or Senri. To this day I can still visualize the memorable scenery from the Hankyu Kyoto line of my youth, like the Suntory Yamazaki Distillery and the concrete factory in Awaji.

In fifth grade, we moved to a Kawanishi, a commuter town just north of Osaka in Hyogo Prefecture. Instead of the Kyoto Line, we were now situated on the Hankyu Takarazuka Line (shared with the Nose—pronounced no-say—Electric Railway) by way of Kawani-shi-noseguchi Station. Whether we were going to Takarazuka, Kobe (Sannomiya Station), Osaka (Umeda Station), or Kyoto (Kawara-machi or Arashiyama Stations), or Mino-o (via the Mino-o Line) or Itami (via the Itami Line), every trip started with the Hankyu Takarazuka Line.

Once I found my first job after college, I rented a small apartment in Kobe's Okamoto neighborhood. The closest station was Okamoto Station on Hankyu's Kobe Line. I also could have used JR's Settsu-Motoyama Station, but for my commute, I chose to stick with the familiar Hankyu lines whenever possible.

Hankyu trains accompanied me through half of my life. For cram school, regular school, work, play, dates, movies, shopping, going on trips, annual New Year's Day shrine visits, going to the airport (via Hotarugaike Station), and visiting home, all of it was by Hankyu. In my mind's eye, that maroon color signifies trains and my youth.

An episodic novel written by Hiro Arikawa utilizes the Hankyu Railway. It is titled, appropriately, *Hankyu Densha*. I purchased the book based on the cover and title alone. At the start of the novel, I was propelled by nostalgia, but before long I was immersed within the story's gentle, almost maternal wistfulness, and I finished reading it at express-train speed.

Hankyu is an odd novel—an ensemble piece set on the Hankyu Imazu Line, a very local-scale line even for Kansai, with a total of only eight stations and a round trip of about half an hour. And the story even eschews rush hour to instead tell a series of everyday episodes. Unlike conventional train novels, *Hankyu* has no murders, no terrorists, and no record-breaking disasters.

The principal characters are women of all ages: an office worker betrayed by her fiancé, a book enthusiast who is ready for romance, an older woman with a complicated relationship with her son and daughter-in-law, a college student with an abusive boyfriend, a middle-aged woman with social anxiety.

At each train station, the narrative's point of view is passed to another character. The women who happen to meet on the train come and go, the tracks of their lives switch, they change speed, and the story departs anew. Across the round trip through every station on the Imazu Line, their individual dramas link together like train cars. Later, each small, seemingly unrelated episode connects into one larger, invigorating tale, and the book serves as a wake-up call for anyone who is rushing through life, as many urban dwellers are. Offered to the modern woman, *Hankyu Densha* exalts a slow train–like life.

Anyone who reads this book—even if they don't know the Hankyu Railway, let alone have an emotional attachment to it like I do—will absolutely want to ride a Hankyu-line train. From commuters sick and tired of being packed into trains day in and day out, to people who don't typically ride trains at all, the reader will surely want to share in the experience of the railway in this book—to ride without urgency, to see once-remembered city scenery, to feel the warmth of people around them, and to notice the subtle, mundane moments of life.

This February, I detoured from a business trip to pay a visit to my father's grave near my old house. I rode the Hankyu Railway for the first time in a year. I didn't know anyone on the train, and the view that passed by the window had changed greatly since I had lived there. The interior of the train car had been remodeled and made high-tech. But even then, the ride felt nostalgic amid the train's cozy, cradle-like sway. For me, the Hankyu Railway is not just a means of getting from one place to another, but a time machine connecting my memories to my hometown.

Hankyu Densha made me realize that trains connect more than geographic regions; they are themselves memes that bridge our many generations.

Hankyu Densha (Hankyu Railway)
Written by Hiro Arikawa and published by Gentosha in *papyrus* magazine in 2007 and as a book in January 2008. As of this writing, it has not been translated into English.

Sixteen stories woven from people who happen to encounter each other on a train.

Hankyu Densha takes place along the eight stops (a scant fifteen minutes each way) on the Hankyu Imazu Line and depicts episodic stories of budding romance and looming separation, along with the subtleties of human relationships, with a richness of humor and pathos. The first chapter is a boy-meets-girl story that begins with a library book. You can build a picture of a person from the books they read. Maybe it's possible that sharing the same taste in books can make it easy for two people to fall in love. ■

SOME PLACES NEED TO BE KNOWN BY EVERY JAPANESE PERSON

***Orgel* (Music Box)**
Written by Minato Shukawa

March 11, 2011, 2:46 p.m. At a magnitude 9.0, the fourth-largest ever recorded earthquake struck approximately twenty-four kilometers below the ocean's surface off the Sanriku coast. More than 14,000 people lost their lives in a tsunami the likes of which had never been experienced before. Another 13,804 remain missing, and some 16,000 people are still living in evacuation shelters. (The numbers are accurate as of April 20, 2011, 10 a.m.)

How are we supposed to respond to such an unprecedented disaster? How can we come to grips with the suffering of those who have been robbed of their futures? How should we survivors go on living our lives?

It was in the haze of these thoughts that I read Minato Shukawa's *Orgel*.

Minato Shukawa is among my favorite authors. He is especially good at writing stories set in Tokyo's working-class areas in the late '50s and early '60s. His style is often called nostalgic horror. Like me, he was born in 1963 and raised in Osaka, and readers of my generation who grew up in Kansai, western Japan, are especially likely to cry while reading his books.

To be honest with you, my original plan for this essay was to introduce one of Shukawa's standout short stories ("Tokabi no Yoru" from *Hana Manma*, "Ippen-san" from *Ippen-san*, or "Shiori no Koi" from *Katami Uta*). I would have, had March 11 not happened.

After the earthquake, I was looking through the heap of books that had tumbled from my bookshelves when I happened to find *Orgel*.

Orgel is considerably different from Shukawa's typical nostalgic Showa era works like *Hana Manma*.

> *The kanji for person (人) consists of a long line leaning against a shorter line, as if the shorter line is supporting the other with all its might. Even if both are supporting each other, it is not in fair measure; the stronger bosses the weaker, and the weaker spends its entire existence in forced hardship.*
>
> *It's like Hitomi always says—there are winners and there are losers. And I'm the son of a loser.*

That was from a candid internal monologue from the main character, a boy named Hayato, from the opening chapter. Hayato is a fourth-grade elementary student who lives in a dilapidated public apartment building with his mom, Hitomi, who firmly refuses to pay for his overdue school lunch fees. His father was a whistleblower and consequently lost his job, and ultimately his marriage. In front of Hayato, Hitomi openly denigrates his father as "a loser." An insidious brand of bullying is rampant in his classroom, and Hayato himself is complicit. Absent are Showa-era nostalgia and the admirable virtues that bolstered Japan's rapid postwar growth. This is a story of the cruel reality of Heisei-era Japan, paralyzed, having hit the peak of prosperity and stagnating there.

> *"I want you to deliver something to my friend who lives in Kagoshima."*

One day, Tonda, an old man who lives in the apartment complex, asks Hayato to deliver a music box to the only person in the entire world who can hear its music. But the boy uses the 20,000-yen train fare to buy a portable video game system instead. Sometime later, the old man is discovered dead, having passed away with no one to notice. Heavy with guilt, Hayato uses his spring break to fulfill his broken promise. Along his journey, adults tell him the following:

> *"No matter how terrible the tragedy, many of us must come bear witness with our own eyes and never forget, else we do the departed an injustice."*

> *"That accident is not something to be dismissed as simply a matter of the past. People all over Japan need to witness the place it happened and etch it into their hearts."*

> *"My dad used to tell me and my brother it's a parent's duty to take us to see Hiroshima and Nagasaki."*

The Great Hanshin Earthquake, the location of the Amagasaki derailment, the Hiroshima Peace Memorial Museum, the Chiran Peace Museum—as Hayato meets adults bearing many traumas, his trip to deliver the music box becomes a pilgrimage of what was left behind after the losses of life to disaster, accident, and war. In time, he realizes that what is important is not the division of winners and losers, but to listen attentively to the ties between people and time, and life and death.

Orgel is a coming-of-age story; Hayato grows from being unwilling to listen to the concerns of adults, to being able to feel empathy for their sorrows (to hear their timbre). Of Shukawa's works, this is the first I've read that has tried to bridge the current Heisei era into the future.

In this moment, we are being tested. And the rest of the world is watching us to see if Japan can once again pull off a miracle.

And in this test—this disaster—what can we do? How will we create bridges into the future? We are being asked to prove our merit. Even if a meme can only be heard by one person, each and every one of us should attempt to listen, and then pass it on to the world, just as Tonda trusted Hayato to do.

Those connections are another music box—one that has been entrusted to us.

■ MAY 2011

Orgel (Music Box)
Written by Minato Shukawa and published by Kodansha in October 2010. As of this writing, the novel has not been translated into English.

On a journey to deliver a music box to Kagoshima, a fourth-grade boy undergoes great change.

Written by Naoki Award–winning author Minato Shukawa, *Orgel* is the heartwarming and sometimes tear-bringing story of Hayato, a boy in fourth grade who goes on a cross-country journey from Tokyo to Kagoshima. Hayato visits places linked to mass losses of life, including the site of a terrible train accident, the Atomic Bomb Dome, and a military base from which kamikaze pilots launched— places which "every Japanese person must know." The story of Hayato's emotional growth provides us gentile guidance for how we should come to grips with the Great East Japan earthquake and how we should now act. ■

I MUST GO PAST NATIONAL AND CULTURAL BOUNDARIES AND CREATE MY OWN WORLD

Satori
Written by Don Winslow

Most every boy has wished at some point or another to become a man with *shibumi*, a suave and detached type of being cool. But what I wanted was not just any kind of *shibumi*. I aspired to be a man who had completely mastered *shibumi*. *Shibumi* is also the title of a thrilling and fun novel about Nicholai Hel, an active operative of the CIA who was raised by a Japanese general and armed with an Eastern mentality and a mastery of his *ki*. The author went by the pseudonym Trevanian and passed away in 2005. *Shibumi* is a landmark spy novel beloved by readers worldwide, and Trevanian (an American) accurately depicts the distinctively Japanese mentality of *wabi*, *sabi*, and *shibumi*, which even native Japanese people have trouble fully understanding. When I was still a schoolboy who only gave his attention to Western novels, it was *Shibumi* that introduced me to the old Japanese concept of its title.

Whether by simple coincidence or not, the *Metal Gear Solid* series shares several major similarities to *Shibumi*'s world. CQC, the cutting-edge martial art adopted in *MGS3*, has commonalities with the naked/kill discipline described in *Shibumi*. When I underwent scout/tracking training in preparation for MGS4, I learned about concepts of awareness and baselines (which the game visualizes as a "threat ring" that encircles the player character). This notion of heightened, almost ninja-like senses was reminiscent of Hel's "proximity sense"—so much so that I was startled when I later re-read *Shibumi* in 2006 as part of my research. My reappraisal of the novel led me to recommend it to the development team. *Shibumi* also includes a merciful murder, an idea hard to understand for a Westerner, where the main character kills his parent from a place of genuine love. That same spirit of dignity and compassion resonates with the stories of *MGS*'s father (Big Boss) and mother (The Boss).

This April, *Satori*, a prequel to *Shibumi*, was published, written by popular author Don Winslow. But could he bring out that uniquely Trevanian sensibility? Much like the other *Shibumi* fans all around the world, it was with a tinge of unease that I opened *Satori*.

> *Nicholai Hel watched the maple leaf drop from the branch, flutter in the slight breeze, then fall gently to the ground.*
> *It was beautiful.*

Those are the first two sentences, and what emotionality and beauty that opening contains. Then, on the second page:

> *It was the nature of a maple leaf to drop in the autumn. I killed General Kishikawa, as close to a father as I ever had, because it was my filial nature—and duty—to do so.*

Well now, in the description of the maple leaves, Winslow opens his novel with a declaration—this book does indeed carry on *Shibumi*'s spirit. Within just the first two pages, my banal apprehensions were swept away. And then the pacing is incredible. The writing is incredibly visual, like a movie. The opera house assassination scene played in my mind with moving pictures and sound. It's like a storyboard ready to be made into a movie. The plot is extremely simple and follows, brilliantly, the tried-and-true spy novel pattern: briefing, infiltration, torture, escape, betrayal, reversal, counterattack. But rather than be disinteresting, the plot propelled me straight through to the finish.

And perhaps the most crucial *shibumi* element of Trevanian's *Shibumi*—the extensive knowledge of the Japanese person—is every bit as present and astute, even in little details that we are often not conscious of doing ourselves, like how we walk with our hands crossed behind our back so as not to inconvenience the people walking past us from the other direction.

> *"Ah...what Go is to philosophers and warriors, chess is to accountants and merchants."*

That line is spoken by Nicholai in *Shibumi*, but *Satori* presents many occasions when clandestine warfare is approached with a Go player's mentality.

> *You play your chess game, I will play Go.*

This one is from Nicholai in *Satori*. The Go-mind versus chess-mind battle between him and his chessmaster target, Voroshenin, is fresh and exciting.

When I come across a blue-eyed character like Nicholai Hel, who is more Japanese-like than a Japanese person in some ways, it makes me wonder how Japanese *I* am.

After the Tohoku earthquake, I received a common message from both fans and associates from places around the world. "For the good of the world, you need to leave Japan and make something. To spend your life and resources on rebuilding your past is the wrong decision." But I did not leave Japan. In my head, I couldn't separate my own purpose from Japan's reconstruction. That's when I realized it: as much as I think of myself as a cosmopolitan person, my substance is and always has been innately Japanese. I immediately began to ask myself questions: "Who am I?" "For whom am I creating?" I had brought myself to a standstill, unable to move. In *Satori*, there is a scene between two freethinkers, neither of the East nor the West (Nicholai, who was born and raised in Asia, and de Lhandes, who was born and raised in the West) exchange their views of their future.

> *"We are both forever on the outside looking in," Nicholai said. "So we can either stand on the periphery of their world, always looking in, or we can create our own."*

He's right. I'm not Western. I'm not Eastern. I'm not Japanese. I'm Hideo Kojima. Because the games I make are played across national and cultural boundaries, I'm sometimes called "*Sekai no Kojima*," meaning "Kojima of the World." But there's no need to let myself be so confounded by some nickname. The only thing I need to do is create my own world—the world of Hideo Kojima. Sharing that with the rest of the world is my karma.

I made up my mind. I don't need a *satori* (epiphany). I will bear my karma and go on living with it.

■ JULY 2011

Satori
Written by Don Winslow, based on Trevanian's Shibumi, and published by Hachette in March 2011. Translated into Japanese by Toshiyuki Kurohara and published (in two volumes) by Hayakawa in April 2011.

Shibumi's vision resonates with the Metal Gear Solid *series.*

Tokyo, 1951. The solitary assassin from Trevanian's *Shibumi* is being held in Sugamo Prison until the CIA sends him to Peking on a covert mission. There, he is to assassinate a KGB commissioner to foment hostility between China and the Soviets, until....

Satori breaks new ground after the action novels of the aughts. ■

.

I REALIZED DATURA IS RIGHT HERE; I HAD BEEN MAKING IT WITH MY OWN HAND

Coin Locker Babies
Written by Ryu Murakami and translated by Stephen Snyder

As a child, lemons were the only bomb I could get. Just like the destitute protagonist in Motojiro Kajii's "The Lemon" left a "terrible, shining golden bomb" in the high-class Maruzen bookstore, I would always sneak in a California lemon to places I didn't like and leave it there. Lemons were my ultimate weapon; I could bring them anywhere, only I could operate them, and with them I could blast the world into smithereens at any time or place I wanted to.

In high school, I realized that lemon grenades did not in fact have the destructive capacity capable of ending the world. It was then that someone told me about an explosive novel that succeeded "The Lemon." This someone was a childhood friend named Tatsuo (coincidentally, a character in the novel is a Filipino named Tatsuo de la Cruz), and the new weapon he handed to me was not a fruit but a morning glory. And that was how I came upon DATURA.

DATURA:
"Common name 'Korean morning glory'; also called 'crazy eggplant.' Says it 'contains alkaloids that can be poisonous, also

known to cause disorientation, mood swings, even hallucinations. Cultivated in Central and South America (Sp. bolatiero) for important medicinal tropane alkaloids such as atorphine and scopolamine.'"

My friend opened the novel to a page with a bookmark and acted out a line spoken by a character named Gazelle. "I you want to destroy everything, it's a magic spell, DATURA. If you want to kill 'em all, DATURA." Then he added, "It's cool," then pressed the book into my chest and left.

The novel he lent me had just been published. It was Ryu Murakami's first full-length third-person novel, *Coin Locker Babies*.

I devoured that book without stopping to drink or eat. The prose, though vulgar, radiated a furious energy, not fitting into sounds or pictures or anything I'd ever experienced before. My stomach whirled. My ears pounded. My heart banged about inside my chest. My head swam. I felt warm between my legs. Several times, I felt like I might puke. This book violated me, wounded me, and fiercely clutched me tight. Ravaged by its brutal caress, for the first time I perceived the necessity of a bomb that could destroy the world.

In the novel, DATURA represents a weapon of mass destruction. One of the main characters, Hashi, is a vocalist in a band, and his bandmate says to him:

"You're in a league by yourself; who else you ever heard could crawl inside people's heads and stroke their brains? You're like some kind of drug. But a drug's just not enough when it comes to getting an audience worked up. You need a bomb for that—a bomb that'll blow away all the daydreams your drug produces in a few seconds."

That's it! A bomb that can blow away everything in an instant! It's DATURA, and that destructive impulse is the rock-and-roll soul coursing through this book. I'm not an anarchist. I'm not a libertarian. I was merely a disciple of Rock.

Rock is a rejection of the existing rules, a resistance against dragging along the past, an act of terrorism to destroy the systems built up by those who came before, and a controller of memes equipping a generation to decide the future.

As for movies, Gakuryu Ishii's *Burst City* and Shinya Tsukamoto's *Tetsuo: The Iron Man* embody this spirit perfectly, as does Katsuhiro Otomo's manga *Akira*. To build a world for the new youth, the existing world is destroyed and the old age is ended. Norms are broken, cities and nations destroyed. Parents, ancestors, and the current inhabitants are killed. To carry memes forward is to bring in the new generation through the massacre of the previous.

"What's DATURA?"
[...]
"The medicine to make Tokyo snow-white," Kiku said.

Coin Locker Babies is a novel of youthful Rock. Without realizing it, my own ethos had become the same as the one from the book. I came to believe that that search for DATURA was the soul of Rock.

But no matter how hard I looked, I never found DATURA anywhere. Eventually I grew up, got a job, got a family, and directed my uncontainable energies into my work and my children. By the will-o'-the-wisp fire that was the bursting of the bubble economy, the world was singed but not destroyed. I thought, with resignation, that the era of Rock had ended and all that was left was to go on with my life.

Thirty years after my first reading, I read *Coin Locker Babies* again. I hadn't understood it before, but Hideo, now in third person, knew: the DATURA that had so long evaded him was right there, and he had been making it with his own hands. Just as Kiku and Anemone spread DATURA across Tokyo at the end of the novel, Hideo was scattering his own DATURA bombs at the world. Hideo's DATURA contains the memes that will birth the new world, and a new him, after he and his world were over.

Hideo closed the book and began to realize that the era of Rock had not yet ended.

We are *Coin Locker Babies*.

Now, wake up. Smash. Kill. Destroy it all.

■ OCTOBER 2011

Coin Locker Babies

Written by Ryu Murakami and published by Kodansha in October 1980. Translated into English by Stephen Snyder and published by Kodansha International in May 1995 and again in May 2013 by Pushkin Press.

A coming-of-age novel of destruction and liberation, erupting with knock-out energy.

Kiku and Hashi were abandoned in coin lockers as babies. A squatter in an abandoned mining town tells Kiku the word "DATURA," and Kiku can't get it out of his mind. Hashi goes to Tokyo in search of his mother, and Hashi follows. There he meets Anemone, a young woman with a pet crocodile. Kiku obtains the DATURA from the bottom of the sea and uses it to "destroy" Tokyo. ■

A FAILURE COMMITTED BY WE HUMAN BEINGS WHO SCORNED NATURE

Virus: The Day of Resurrection
Written by Sakyo Komatsu and translated by Daniel Huddleston

When the Tohoku earthquake struck, I found myself uttering:

Why had it happened, and who was responsible?
What savage presence had visited such a disaster on this lovely
planet?

Seven months later, with the recovery stalling, I again found myself saying:

So who *had caused this disaster? Some solitary madman? Had*
the very organization of human society been responsible? Had
it been caused by someone's mistake? It was already known that
somebody and something caused it.
How did this happen, and why?

Those words are from the prologue to *Virus: The Day of Resurrection*, a 1964 novel written by the Japanese SF giant Sakyo Komatsu. He left us on July 26, 2011, without ever seeing the recovery after the earthquake. He was 80.

The day before his passing, I saw his novel *Japan Sinks* on a special display in the bookstore, and I purchased it. Ironically, it took an earthquake for people to take new notice of his incredible talent. I couldn't help but feel some kind of fate at work.

I wondered what he must have been feeling in the face of this unprecedented disaster. In search of the answer, I reacquired a collection of his works: *Hateshinaki Nagare no Hate Ni* (At the End of the Endless Stream), *Virus: The Day of Resurrection, Tsugu no wa Dare Ka?* (Who Will Inherit?), *Gordian Knot*, and *Kessho Seidan* (Crystal Star Cluster).

If I were to pick his best work, it would have to be *At the End of the Endless Stream*. But when I revisited *Virus*, I was shocked. The story left me feeling completely different than it had when I was a child. The depiction of Yoshizumi confronting the skeletons in Tokyo Bay superimposed with 3/11 in my mind and moved me to tears.

I first read *Virus* in the mid-1970s. By that time, a story about a pandemic caused by germ warfare was hardly unusual. But whenever I think about how the novel was written in 1964, I can't help but still be surprised. Komatsu wrote *Virus* before Michael Crichton's *The Andromeda Strain*, before Koji Tanaka's *Oinaru Tobo* (*The Great Escape*), before George Romero's *The Crazies* (often considered the originator of pandemic movies), and way before George Pan Cosmatos's *The Cassandra Crossing*. *Virus* was so ahead of its time that it suffered the unfortunate fate of being dismissed as genre SF.

The scale of the story is huge. With meticulous scientific investigation, the political climate of the era, and an ensemble cast of characters in places all over the world, *Virus* provides a rich, detailed, and novelistic depiction of the downfall of the human race. Story elements—such as the spike in the price of chicken eggs needed to produce vaccines, riders wearing white masks in an uncrowded train, and a press that has little grasp of the truth—will evoke memories from recent history, like SARS and the swine flu. Reality fills every page. If you read *Virus* now, I don't think you would mistake it for science fiction.

Despite being a Japanese book, most of what we see takes place outside of Japan. It was written during the Cold War, when diplomatic relations and the aviation network were still undeveloped, and the world was far away. And yet Komatsu's works often took on an unusually global scale in a way that was distinctly his. He was still a child when Japan lost the war—the things he had believed in were stolen from him, and he grew up under military occupation. Maybe it was only natural that the young dreamer would call out for an antiwar, antinuclear future, tell stories on a global scale, and become an SF author whose worlds transcended time and space.

Back when I only read SF, I held a grudge against the world and thought, "If this is what we call society, we're better off destroyed." I loved books about apocalypse and downfall. But when I tried facing reality, I saw that I had been wrong. SF was not a tool for escapism. It was a medium created to send a warning call across national and generational boundaries and into the future. Reading *Virus* again at this point in my life, I now perceive Sakyo Komatsu's powerful desire in its pages.

> *"Medical science is used both to save lives and to conduct research into these damnable germ weapons. It's the same story with atom bombs and nuclear energy. The one works to aid humanity, while the other works to strangle it."*

In the story, the world is destroyed twice, first by a rogue biological weapon and then by an earthquake that triggers a postapocalyptic US-Soviet nuclear war. On 3/11, an earthquake, tsunami, and a nuclear accident created a chain of terrible tragedies.

> *Usually when something we call a "major accident" happens, unfortunate coincidences accumulate to a nearly impossible degree, all manner of safety systems fail one after another, and the accident occurs.*

3/11 was not a natural disaster, but a failure committed by a people who, just like the people of this book, scorned nature. But will we ever have our day of resurrection?

> *No, the world we revive must not be like the one before the Great Calamity. We must not resurrect the gods of envy, the gods of hatred and vengeance.*

If that day ever is to come, it will be when humanity decides on a new, untrodden course, one of prosperity, different than the memes of our past. Will not then be our day of resurrection?

■ **OCTOBER 2011**

Virus: The Day of Resurrection
Written by Sakyo Komatsu and published by Hayakawa in 1964.
Translated into English by Daniel Huddleston and published by Haikasoru in December 2012.

A story of a desperate search for a new start after mankind's arrogance brings catastrophe.

A biological weapon known as MM-88 is accidentally released into the wild. The resulting disease spreads across the entire world with astonishing speed and soon extinguishes mankind, save for fewer than 10,000 survivors in Antarctica. Can humanity rebuild?

Virus is a story of grand scope, about the light and dark sides of scientific advancement, and of humanity's swelling greed and arrogance. The afterword in the Japanese first printing by the novel's erudite author is a must-read. *Virus* offers a new direction for Japan and the world. ■

THE LIFE-OR-DEATH STRUGGLE TO PASS ON MEMES—THAT IS SURVIVAL IN THE TRUEST SENSE.

Hyoryu (Castaway)
by Akira Yoshimura

I often hear, "Truth is stranger than fiction," and indeed, many unusual tales have been based on true events.

Among them, I especially like escape stories. This year, I had the pleasure of seeing return screenings of *The Great Escape* and *Papillon* in the theater. Although they're not really escape movies, I've also gone to see new survival movies like *127 Hours*. All are based on true stories of people returning from adversity alive.

I'd like to introduce you to Akira Yoshimura's *Hyoryu*. I heard about the book from another novelist, Naoki Hyakuta, who by coincidence had read my essay on *Papillon* in my series, *70% of My Body Is Made of Movies*, and told me, "If you like survival and escape stories, you've got to read Akira Yoshimura's *Hagoku* (Prison Break) or *Hyoryu*!"

Hyoryu is based on the true story of a shipwreck in the late Edo Period. In 1785, Chohei and three other sailors on a *sengoku bune* trade vessel from Tosa Province (present-day Kochi Prefecture) were caught in a storm at sea, and their ship was destroyed. They drift to Tori-shima, an uninhabited island south of Hachijo-shima with no vegetation or fresh water—not even a small stream or spring. *Hyoryu* tells a story in exacting and instructive detail of their real-life heroic survival, which spanned twelve years on a harsh, volcanic island.

To the other sailors, who are too mired in their attachment to their past life to try to live in their new reality, Chohei says:

> *"This is the situation we're in. What other choice to we have? Let's use our heads and do what we can to stay alive on this island."*

No ships pass the island; there is no hope for rescue. Chohei urges them to adapt to their situation and survive. They kill and eat the island's only animals, the short-tailed albatross, and use their eggshells to collect rainwater. Chohei intuits that the birds are migratory and begins drying their meat to stockpile food for after the birds leave. He shepherds the group with superior drive and insight.

But eventually, the harsh life—including a diet lacking any semblance of diversity and long stretches of time doing nothing but lying around on the floor of a cave—takes its toll, and all the sailors apart from Chohei fall ill and die.

> *"If we don't move our bodies, bad things will happen. Human beings are made to need work."*

Chohei learns to balance his diet with other food, like fish and shellfish, and to work his body in the sunlight. I don't think that lesson is limited to surviving on an uninhabited island; it applies to modern urbanites too. An indolent, aimless life, following only the desires of existence, is not healthy or sustainable.

But what makes *Hyoryu* so engrossing is its two-part structure: in the first half, Chohei discards his past and his humanity to live like an animal, while in the second, he plans his escape to return to living like a person again.

One day, after five years of surviving on the island, six shipwrecked sailors from Satsuma Province (present-day Kagoshima

Prefecture) wash ashore. As the resident authority on survival, Chohei instructs them in how to live. But despite respecting his method of surviving on the island, they resist accepting it as the only way.

> *"Everyone on our ship is over forty. We don't have that much life ahead of us to spare. I want to do whatever I can to escape this island and return to my homeland."*

Upon hearing the older man's determined speech, Chohei suddenly realizes what it truly means to live. What had been the story of a ghost with an instinct for only passive survival transforms into the story of a living man with the active goal of returning home.

> *"We died once. [...] But shouldn't we ghosts pool our strength together, and return to the land of the living?"*

In the novel's latter half, the tone of the survival story changes drastically. The older men of the Satsuma ship not only came with all the tools required to build a boat, but are also highly skilled craftsmen. They're not like Chohei, who had managed to survive only by his physical strength, animal-like intuition, and instinct. They make plaster and use it to construct a reservoir for rainwater. They make sake from adzuki beans. They improvise a bellows from memory. Theirs is now a civilized life, as best as their knowledge can provide. Together with Chohei, undaunted by the island's total lack of natural resources, they build a ship from driftwood. From old nails and an anchor they fashion new nails. They stitch their clothes together into a sail. And in the end, they build, from nothing, a *sengoku bune* that can carry the ten-odd survivors back home.

It's impossible to witness the wits and tenacity of these men, who spend years completing their patchwork ship and attempt to return home alive entirely through their own efforts, and not be moved and inspired.

When Chohei and the others escape Tori-shima, they leave behind the tools and instructions for survival for any future sailors who drift to the same shore. This becomes a message of hope: here were not just survivors, but people who survived and went home. The story leaves us two memes, two meanings of survival: to live through adversity, and to make it back home alive.

If the desire to preserve our species is a survival instinct, then for these men, the role of their "selfish genes" had already been fulfilled. So then why risk their lives to return home? Because they are driven to leave something not just biological, but of their humanity (their memes)—to not just live, but to return to society. The life-or-death struggle, beyond the realm of instinct, to pass on their memes—that is survival in the truest sense.

A story of homecoming is a story of memes being passed on. And so, a novel of survival is more joyous than survival novels.

■ JANUARY 2012

Hyoryu (Castaway)
Written by Akira Yoshimura and first serialized in the Sankei Shimbun in 1975, then published in novel form by Shinchosha in 1976. As of this writing, Hyoryu has not been published in English, but several of Akira Yoshimura's other works are available in English, including Shipwrecks, One Man's Justice, Storm Rider, and On Parole.

A creative-nonfiction novel of a Japanese castaway's survival on an uninhabited island and the escape home, Hyoryu *stands among the masterpieces of the world.*

Don't assume that the West has full reign over adventure and survival novels. Written by famed true-story novelist Akira Yoshimura, *Hyoryu* will likely continue to be read alongside the great works

Robinson Crusoe and *Lord of the Flies*. With absolute realism, *Hyoryu* depicts survival on an uninhabited island, the wide range of emotions felt by its characters, and their passion and resourcefulness that brings them home alive. Yoshimura offers a message: the hope for tomorrow brings people to life. ■

SEPARATE FROM THE CREATION OF ORIGINAL WORK, *OBI* ARE ANOTHER METHOD OF TRANSMITTING MEMES

'*Salem's Lot*'
Written by Stephen King

"Stephen King raves!"

There was a time when all a new translated book needed to fly off the shelves was having those words on the front *obi*, also called a "belly band," which is wrapped around many books sold in Japan.

But lately translated novels have been in a slump, and I hardly ever see that phrase anymore. Even so, when I *do* see those words—"Stephen King raves!"—I'll buy that foreign novel without any further thought.

I'm not what you'd call a Stephen King fan. I've of course seen quite a number of movies based on his novels, but I've read almost none. The only one I read all the way to the end was maybe *The Dark Half*.

Of the big three writers of modern horror (King, Koontz, McCammon), my personal favorite is not King but Robert R. McCammon. Rather than read *The Stand*, I was impressed by its homage, *Swan Song*. I skipped right past what many consider the father of all modern vampire stories,'*Salem's Lot*, and read McCammon's take on vampires, *They Thirst*.

In other words, up until now, I've had more contact with King's blurbs than his novels. I had been reading the writers who followed after King, but not King himself. Oddly enough, I was even a huge fan of Joe Hill, who in 2007 revealed he was King's son.

Last month, a newly revised edition of'*Salem's Lot* was published. The front cover was illustrated by the irresistible-to-modern-horror-fans Shinsaku Fujita. The *obi* contained a wonderful quote from translator Nozomi Omori: "King completely revived a classic monster for modern America."

Naturally, King's own novel didn't have a Stephen King blurb on it. But even just seeing his name in the quote on the *obi* in big block letters, I reflexively purchased the book.

'*Salem's Lot* is considered a groundbreaking novel for reviving the pre-nineteenth-century vampire story into the current era. But the setting, the plot, and the way the vampires work are all quite orthodox. Why then, is the novel so well regarded? Because, like with King's other novels, he has filled the setting with an almost eccentric level of detail and, and in doing so, created a sense of realism.

The setting is a fictional town of 1,300 residents in Maine called Jerusalem's Lot, and the story progresses around the protagonists' fight against the vampires. But with all the interwoven storylines of the people who live in the rural town, I would go as far to say as the town itself is the main character—'*Salem's Lot* has been likened to the vampire version of *Payton Place*. Part of nearly every page is sectioned off, moatlike, by exposition about the town's history, land, residents, and buildings. But even if the narrative takes a wide detour from the main thread, and even if the pacing slows, the wealth of details continues long enough for the reader to have accepted the story's supernatural elements. The thoroughness of the depiction of the setting adds a steady, grounded reality to the fiction. Meanwhile, absolutely no explanation is given for the existence of vampires in this modern era. This is a completely different approach to Matheson's *I Am Legend*, which offers a scientific cause for vampirism (a virus).

One other aspect in which King excels is the montage. I want to call attention to chapter three, which begins, "The town is not slow to wake." The perspective of this chapter is given to the town itself, which depicts a meticulously timed collage starting at 4 a.m. and ending with the claiming of the first victim at 11:59 p.m. Instead of following a primary character through the day, the point of view jumps from one location of the town to another. By moving from scene to scene, from the town's awakening to when it goes to sleep, the chapter provides a dizzying bird's-eye view.

Similarly, the final confrontation is also mesmerizing. The time is mentioned somewhere in each chapter, and each time, sundown is that much closer. Refilling the gasoline, 5:15. Parting with the constable, 5:30. Preparing the holy water, 5:45. Arriving at home base, 6:10. The cellar, 6:23. Root cellar, 6:40. Coffin, 6:45. Vampire, 6:51. Confrontation, 6:53. And sunset, 6:55. See, you're worried about the time. Your palms are sweating. It's hard to breathe. You want to close the book, but your body, as if under the vampire's control, keeps turning the pages. You feel like you're being sucked into a bottomless swamp. This is why Stephen King is called the king of page-turners.

Though I came to it late, the revised edition of *'Salem's Lot* sank its fangs into my heart and made me King's prisoner—no, make that his *thrall*.

Lately, I've been getting asked more frequently to provide cover blurbs for people's books. Of course, that's not as praiseworthy as being an author, but if my *obi* can stare at you with a vampire's gaze and lure you toward a book, isn't that itself another fine way to pass along memes?

I would never have been able to recommend books through this series in *Da Vinci* if it weren't for encounters with King on the *obi*. Separate from the creation of original work, *obi* are another method of conveying memes, and I suppose they too are among my lovable memes.

■ **FEBRUARY 2012**

'Salem's Lot

Written by Stephen King and published by Doubleday in October 1975, with an illustrated edition with additional material published as a limited edition in November 2004, and again by Doubleday in December 2005. Translated into Japanese by Jun Nagai and published by Shueisha in May 1983, with a revised edition in November 2011.

A vampire story offering a detailed depiction of a peaceful town slowly consumed by terror.

A small American town is shaken by a string of mysterious incidents—and a second coming of vampires is to blame. The creeping sense of terror is primordial, and yet still present and close. Some readers keep a respectful distance from Stephen King because they think his books are too long, but in order to truly savor the thrill of the tumultuous twists and turns at the very end, you have to let the author's thorough and careful presentation sink into you. ■

THE JOY OF FINDING AND THE CATHARSIS OF GOING TO GREAT TROUBLE IN SEARCHING FOR SOMETHING AND FINDING IT

I Spy (series)
Photographs by Walter Wick and riddles by Jean Marzollo

Last Christmas, I bought a picture book for my child. It was the Christmas installment of *I Spy*, a series of hidden-object books. The moment I opened the book, its pictures transformed my surroundings into a world of silver. And that was what brought me to *I Spy*; I purchased the book without really understanding anything about it. But then both parent and child were hooked.

After that we did *I Spy* together practically every night. When we finished solving the first book, I bought another, and then another, and so on. By the beginning of this year, we had collected the entire series. (Just be careful of shameless copycat books.)

Play one riddle and you'll immediately see why *I Spy* is so captivating. Although *Where's Waldo* and *I Spy* are both hidden-object books, the latter is something completely different. With *Waldo*, you are given specific characters and objects to find, for which you are shown examples, making the game not unlike a spot-the-differences riddle. But in *I Spy*, the reader is given not pictures but word clues. For example: frogs. What kind of frogs? What color? How big are they? Are they toys? Are they drawings? You have to keep following that line of questions and prowl through the book until you find all the kinds of frogs there are. If you come into the search bringing a specific notion of "frogs," you may never find one. You have to discard your preconceptions and find the frogs that are there—that's the unique pleasure of *I Spy*.

Sometimes what you're searching for might be buried in snow, or is a shadow, or is a reflection, or is hazy, or is a part of a bridge or building, or is hidden just perfectly across the picture's edge. The objects are all sizes. This is a toy world, so not everything is its natural size. To find what you're looking for, you have to shift your internal sense of scale at will.

I Spy isn't a set of questions to guide the player to the answers, and it's not a typical game or puzzle book that seeks to make you compete for a score. As if to prove the point, *I Spy* doesn't even include the answers anywhere. Every book in the series follows that rule. The creators also go a step further, replacing what might have been the answer pages with a variety of clever bonus challenges, such as extra-credit riddles, or a prompt to help the players to make up their own. *I Spy* is a delightful invention, allowing the game to be played both alone or with a child; it can be played however you like, as many times as you like.

Each page is jam-packed with a motley assortment of odds and ends, almost as if a toy box has been dumped out, and the objects will inspire interest in children and nostalgia in adults. The treasure hoard was personally collected by the series' photographer from antique shops around the globe and includes toys such as dolls, marbles, toy cars, stuffed animals, and more; found objects, such as bird feathers, shells, and nuts; treats, such as candy and cookies; and familiar stationery, such as scissors and paperclips—all objects that a child might stash in a drawer. I think the use of these props in every photograph is why each turn of the page fills the reader with such a pleasant feeling.

The sharpness of your vision is irrelevant; I get plenty of enjoyment even with my old eyes. You don't need good squinting muscles. The main point is to see through the subtle tricks and misleads that photographer designed into the photos. This is a battle of wits, fought with the mind, not the eyes.

We live in the era of the search engine. Gone is the era of finding things on your own. If you want to find something, you can use your computer or phone to easily google it. You can find popular stores, restaurants, movies, novels, and fashion anywhere in the world with no challenge. Ours is now a life of passive acquisition. But the joy of finding is gone, as is the catharsis of going to great trouble in searching for something and finding it. That's why I want to recommend *I Spy*. From a cornucopia of odds and ends, search for and find the treasure you need—and cultivate the degree of discernment you'll need to do so. Within that polished eye, memes are waiting. Through these books, I've gained experience in finding things for myself, experience that will be put to positive work. When it does, I'll be grateful to myself for spying *I Spy*.

All of life is hide and seek.
If you open your eyes
Your heart will also peek.
Get with the rhythm and the rhyme
Find your memes with your eyes
Now go play I Spy!

■ **MARCH 2012**

I Spy (series)

Photographs by Walter Wick and riddles by Jean Marzollo. The first book, *I Spy: A Book of Picture Riddles*, was published by Scholastic in April 1992, translated into Japanese by Shigesato Itoi, and published by Shogakukan starting in August 1992.

I have every book in the series.

I recommend *I Spy 7: Treasure Hunt* and *Can You See What I See? Treasure Ship*. The dioramas in *Treasure Ship* took nine months to stage and are a delight; it is also the entry with the most effective visual tricks and misleads. For each diorama in *Treasure Ship*, the camera is zoomed out from the previous one, and the use of that filmlike technique is another reason why it's my favorite. ∎

I HEARD MY OWN FATHER'S VOICE, SHELTERED WITHIN ME ALL ALONG

Hoshiyadori no Koe
(The Voices of the Hoshiyadori Café)
Written by Ryo Asai

It was the summer of Showa 52, the year 1977. The pop idol trio Candies had just announced they were retiring. My father, Kingo, who worked at a pharmaceutical company, came home unusually early from work and complained that he had a headache. My mother and I were the only ones home. My older brother was still at school with extracurriculars. My mom was cooking an early dinner when suddenly I heard a loud cry. I looked over and saw my dad on the floor, convulsing. His skin was blue, thanks to cyanosis. I called the emergency number 119, left my distressed mother inside, and went out front to direct the ambulance. I could hear the siren in the darkening sky. With only a few towels and my wallet, I climbed into the ambulance and rode to the ER.

"Mr. Kojima, can you hear me? Kingo Kojima? Can you understand me?"

The EMT repeatedly tried to determine whether my dad was conscious or not, but my dad couldn't answer. He just kept looking at me through his convulsions. His eyes looked like they were trying to tell me something. The next evening, without having been able to leave a will, my father passed away. It was an acute subarachnoid hemorrhage. He was 45. I was 13.

Father is in a photograph we keep on a white shelf, and inside a white box.

I don't know what he was trying to tell me back then. I've gone my whole life thinking about and carrying that question.

"Ama-yadori" is when you take shelter from the rain. And so when Father put a small skylight in the ceiling of his coffee shop to catch light of the fragile stars, he called it the "Hoshi-yadori."

With *Hoshiyadori no Koe*, the young novelist Ryo Asai has already penned a masterpiece. The setting is a fictional seaside city called Rengahama (reminiscent of real-life Kamakura), and depicts the growth and bonds of a large family: the mother, Ritsuko, who manages the café left behind by her husband Hoshinori, an architect who died of cancer four years previous; eldest daughter Kotomi (fourth year in the workforce); eldest son Mitsuhiko (a fourth-year college student); twin daughters Koharu and Ruri (third-year students in senior high); second son Ryoma (a first-year student in senior high); and third son Maho (a sixth-grade elementary school student). This might have been the beginning of a commonplace family drama, but it's not. The prose shimmers with delicately crystalized perceptivity, and Asai episodically switches the story's point of view with a uniquely deft hand, reinforcing the novel's theme of the generational passing of the torch.

It wasn't snowing, but the outside world appeared starkly white; not an untouched white, but a white that had been put there to paper over all those things that were now beyond control.

Asai employs white imagery symbolically throughout the novel. Pure white milk, curtains, architectural design notes—all are in the father's favorite color. A stark white hospital room, bed, and patient's gown; in a season of white, a man is put in white clothes, and is returned to white; white is the last color he leaves behind. Black imagery also makes frequent appearances in contrast: the beef stew on the café's featured menu, the drip coffee, the mourners' clothing, the children's school uniforms. Even the coastal town is likened to curry rice when viewed from above. Despite being set on the seaside, the novel's colors are restrained in monochromatic coordination.

The colors begin to change when a regular customer, Old Man Brown (nicknamed for the brown cardigan he always wears) stops coming to the café. With his color absent, the family finally notices the other colors they've lost. The twins dream of becoming color coordinators, the eldest daughter works at a jewelry store with all manner of colorful jewels, and the youngest son loves to take pictures to capture his family's full colors on film. Together they search for the right new colors for their family as they repaint their own hues onto the white-colored family tree left by their father Hoshinori's passing. Put another way, *Hoshiyadori* is the story of a family, having lost their pillar and had their colors mixed to a homogenous gray, learning how to reset their color balance and exposure. At first glance, each section, told from the perspective of a different child, might appear disjointed from the others, but then the baton is expertly passed to the next, until finally they show their beautiful, miraculous harmony beneath the café's star-shaped skylight—the meme Hoshinori left to them.

"Father wanted to show you so much more, tell you so much more, teach you so much more. He wanted to see you go off somewhere beyond this town."

On that summer day, I was convinced that by losing my father in body, I'd lost him. But I was wrong. He is still inside me. I carry his voice within me; that is what he wanted to tell me back then. Within this book, I heard his voice, which had been sheltered within me for thirty-five years.

"Look after them."

Sometime, the day will come when I will pass my torch, my memes, on to my children. When that time comes, I will look to them in that same way, and they will know.

Everything will be all right because you are my children.

■ **APRIL, 2012**

Hoshiyadori no Koe
(The Voices of the Hoshiyadori Café)
Written by Ryo Asai and published by Kadokawa in June 2014. As of this writing, the novel has not been translated into English.

A mother and her three sons and three daughters in a town over-looking the sea, and the miracle their father left behind for them.

Hoshiyadori no Koe is the story of six siblings with their own feelings and conflicts living in a seaside town as they begin to take their first steps toward their future. The novel expresses its memes through many forms and objects—from the region and scenery to even the colors. In 2001, while he was still attending Waseda University, Ryo Asai won the twenty-second Shosetsu Subaru Prize for New Writers with his novel *Kirishima Says He's Quitting the Team*. *Hoshiyadori no Koe* was his graduation thesis. ■

MINAGAWA'S SHARP-WITTED SCALPEL OPENED MY CHEST AND MY HEART WITH THE FEELING OF ONLY PLEASURE

Dilated to Meet You (The Resurrection Fireplace)
Written by Hiroko Minagawa and translated by Matt Treyvaud

> *"If it were done when 'tis done, then 'twere well it were done quickly,"* recited Clarence. Macbeth. *He bowed to the boy's corpse.* "Dilated to meet you," *he said solemnly.*

At the end of last year, the 2012 edition of the annual guide-book, *Kono Mystery ga Sugoi!* (These mysteries are excellent!) was published. Though I may not be as interested in the rankings as I once was, I still want to know—not to find new books, but to see if the books—the memes—I'd already chosen for myself were on the list.

Topping the domestic list was *Genocide*. I'd read an advance copy and had the good fortune of being asked to write a blurb for the *obi* band around the book. Number two was *Oreta Ryukotsu* (Broken Keel) by Honobu Yonezawa. I hadn't read that one, but I'd finished every novel in the author's Classic Literature Club series. With a prideful smirk I thought, *My antennae aren't too shabby.* But on the next title, I froze. *The Resurrection Fireplace?* The author was Hiroko Minagawa. I'd heard the name before, but I hadn't read any of her books. My pride as a daily browser of bookstores was deeply wounded.

Who is this writer? Wound still stinging, I googled her and came across an interview.

The eighty-one-year-old author goes to a bookstore every day. "I don't like to take walks outside, so I at least walk inside a bookstore," said Minagawa. Even if she won't get to reading it immediately, when a book catches her eye, she acquires it.
— Asahi Shimbun Digital, *October 21, 2011*

I was shocked. Minagawa—now eighty-two—was of my mom's generation and an active veteran writer.

Without hesitation, I delightedly opened the girls' manga–styled cover of *The Resurrection Fireplace.* Minagawa's sharp-witted scalpel opened my chest and my heart to the pleasure of reading her novels. And then, as if in an anesthetized stupor, I continued straight on to her most famous works, *Shi no Izumi* (Fountain of Death) and *Toritsu Suru To no Satsujin* (Murder at the Upside-Down Tower).

Each novel is a mystery at its core, but they also contain other elements—fantasy, homoerotic, historical, and erotica. Her novels blend fantasy and history, grotesquery and eroticism, transgression and immorality. She put me on her operating table and intoxicated me with the beauty of her interweaving contrasts.

The Resurrection Fireplace is a pop-styled *honkaku* puzzle mystery set in eighteenth-century London with a theme of illegal autopsies. *Shi no Izumi* is a story of revenge and of the love between a parent and child set in a Nazi human-experimentation facility during World War II. *Toritsu Suru To no Satsujin* is a light novel–esque inverted mystery where falsehoods and truth intertwine in a missionary school in postwar Tokyo.

Each is packed with meticulous research, the author's own experiences and knowledge, her imagination, authorial voice, and point of view. Minagawa is not an internist prescribing separate pills; she is a surgeon, suturing together foreign art, music, and literature, and firmly binding them. Her stories are epic poems performed with a rich aesthetic beauty.

Moreover, Minagawa's works are an ultimate expression of the character-driven story, in the fashion of girls' manga from the 1970s. Her contemporaries, Tatsuhiko Shibusawa (born 1928), Yukio Mishima (born 1925), and others did much to disseminate transgressive and nonheteronormative memes, which in turn influenced the Year 24 Group—the next generation of creators, such as Moto Hagio, Keiko Takemiya, and Yumiko Oshima, who fueled the boom of girls' manga containing themes of same-sex or otherwise forbidden or transgressive romance. Though Mishima and Shibusawa had gone, the women of the Year 24 Group were passing the baton forward to the young authors of the Heisei era, the late '80s and beyond.

With my chest opened bare, I began to search for Minagawa's earlier novels. Walking from one major bookstore to another, I managed to find her short story collection *Cho* (Butterfly) but no others. It seems like her books don't get reprinted much. Maybe today's readers shy away from stories of the unusual set in foreign countries. The reading and comprehension of unfamiliar cultures, customs, regions, time periods, and beliefs requires effort and stamina from the reader.

The sad truth is that, whether translated or written by Japanese authors, unconventional stories set in foreign counties do not currently sell. What are popular are novels of the ordinary, of the commonplace, of the current times—stories in which anyone can immerse themselves. That wasn't true for our generation. By reading translated stories, we made efforts to understand unfamiliar worlds, cultures, and ideologies. We learned an intellectual excitement for the unknown, because that is what would expose us to new worlds.

That, more than anything, is where the true pleasure of reading is found. Be that as it may, Minagawa's themes of other countries, other worlds, wars, and gender, are intimidating for present-day youth to approach.

Nevertheless, at age eighty-two, Minagawa is still actively extending the baton to twenty-first-century readers. I find that hugely inspiring.

Twenty-five years ago, I incorporated a story and a message into video games—two elements largely considered unnecessary. Now, with the sudden rise of mobile gaming, the trend is reversing. It may be that the times have come to a conclusion: "Video games should be for killing time. They will not rise to the level of being culture."

But even I intend on continuing to as I am now, even after I pass eighty. I will instill my memes into video games. That is the baton Minagawa passed on to me.

Hiroko Minagawa, thank you, truly, for opening my eyes.

And—though I should have said this earlier—Mom, I'm delighted to have met you.

■ MAY 2012

Dilated to Meet You (The Resurrection Fireplace)
Written by Hiroko Minagawa and published by Hayakawa in July 2011. Translated into English by Matt Treyvaud and published by Bento Books in March 2019.

A professor of dissection and his students get caught up in a whirlwind mystery set in 18th century London.

For readers new to Minagawa's works, I recommend starting with *The Resurrection Fireplace*, also known as *Dilated to Meet You* in Japan, for its availability, ease of reading, and because it's immensely entertaining. The setting is eighteenth-century London, in a classroom where human dissections are studied away from the eyes of the law. The mystery begins when the body of a baronet's daughter is inexplicably swapped with that of a boy with amputated limbs. *The Resurrection Fireplace* is a mystery overflowing with Georgian London atmosphere and the author's distinctive humor and aesthetics. ■

WOULD WE BE ABLE TO GO ON LIVING IN SOMEONE ELSE'S LANGUAGE?

The Notebook, The Proof, The Third Lie
Written by Ágota Kristóf

> *What would my life have been like if I hadn't left my country?*
> *More difficult, poorer, I think, but also less solitary, less torn.*
> —The Illiterate, *Ágota Kristóf*

One year after 3/11, I still haven't been able to dispel my anxieties after the massive earthquake and the radioactive contamination. We could lose Japan as a nation. I could lose my sense of belonging as a Japanese person. For a year I've harbored these haggard feelings. But what does it truly mean to lose one's homeland?

It was amid these thoughts that I remembered Ágota Kristóf's *The Notebook*. She was born in Hungary in 1935. In 1956, as a refugee of the Hungarian Revolution, she fled to Switzerland by way of Austria, and lived in French-speaking Neuchâtel until her death in 2011. There, she learned French and became a refugee writer, writing in a language that was not of her birth.

■ Our *The Notebook*
Kristóf's debut novel was published in 1986. *The Notebook* is set in a village bordering Austria in which the author had lived during the tail end of World War II. The protagonists are twins who have been evacuated from the Big Town to live with their grandmother.

Everyone but the twins calls her the Witch. The novel tells, through the first person "we," the story of the young and innocent twins as they tenaciously survive in the war-torn country. The prose is written without the slightest iota of sentimentality. The twins are keeping a strictly factual record of events in their notebook and re-write an entry any time it includes anything but a faithful representation of facts. Consequently, the writing style is extremely simple and acutely objective. When read only on its own, *The Notebook* is a striking work of literary fiction that depicts the absurdity of the twins' cool-headed survival through a time of war.

■ Lucas and Claus's *The Proof*

But then *The Proof* shocked everyone two years later. The second novel is now written in third-person—"we" has become "Lucas" and "Claus." *The Proof* follows chronologically after the first novel. The inseparable twin brothers are split apart on opposite sides of the border. Lucas has been left behind and is continuing to write in the notebook as a diary. But in the end, the novel reveals that Lucas and Claus are anagrams, and the novel's narrator, Lucas, never existed; the notebook was a fabrication, written by Claus alone. "Their" relentlessly factual notebook is retroactively overwritten and repudiates the proof of there ever being twins at all.

■ My *The Third Lie*

Then came *The Third Lie* in 1991, and readers were in for another shock. The trilogy's final novel is told in first person singular. Not only that, this new work gradually reveals that our previous narrators ("We," "Lucas," and "Claus") had all been creations of the narrator's fantasy. This third writer confesses to rewriting the children's text into his own autobiographical fable, as if to assert that it was *his* experienced truth.

From the many-layered construction created by this third lie, Kristóf's own profound feeling of loss becomes revealed. *We* crossed the border and were split into two people, Lucas and Claus. Then,

I, an empty shell cast off into a foreign country, am unable to adapt to *my* new land, but can neither find a place for *myself* in *my* native land. Forced to carry multiple ID cards, *I* do not belong to any people; *I* become a nomad. Even if all of those separate people could be reunited back to *me*, *I* would never again be the *we* who *I* once was. With the reading of each book, the reader's impressions are transformed. No trilogy written before or since has possessed such an acrobatic composition.

During the Great War, the German army occupied Kristóf's village and forced the residents to use the German language. Upon liberating Hungary, the Soviets made learning Russian compulsory in school. In this way, Kristóf's mother tongue was repeatedly stolen from her amid the ravages of war. As a result, she wrote in what she often called "an enemy language," and when she wrote these three novels, she elevated the tragic loss of her native language into literature.

What does it mean to lose one's native language? Japan has no official language because there is nearly only one language. To the Japanese people, our language is our identity. Losing our state or country through war or disaster would be one thing, but if we lost the Japanese language—our nationality—would we be able to go on living in someone else's?

We face the danger of losing our country. Our state could collapse as soon as tomorrow, but I want to believe that Japan could recover. And in order to strengthen that resolve, we all should read Ágota Kristóf's compositions and memes once more.

■ JUNE 2012

The Notebook, The Proof, The Third Lie

Written in French by Ágota Kristóf and published by Seuil in 1986, 1988, and 1991 respectively. Translated into Japanese by Shigeki Hori and published by Nochi in 1991, 1991, and 1992. Grove Press has published English translations of all three novels, with Alan Sheridan's *The Notebook* in 1988, David Watson's *The Proof* in 1991, and Marc Romano's *The Third Lie* in 1996, and a collection of all three in one volume in 1997.

We can read books.
We can write them too.
Stories fill our world.

I hope that you will at least try the easy-to-read *The Notebook*. If you like it, I hope you would continue to *The Proof* and *The Third Lie*. Then, if you are interested, I hope you would read Ágota Kristóf's fourth novel, *Yesterday*, and her memoir, *The Illiterate*. You should find that her sadness is expressed all the more directly when veiled in fiction. When writing this essay, I read all of her novels again straight through. ∎

EVEN IF I HAVE TO ABANDON EVERYTHING ELSE, I HAVE TO CONTINUE

The Summit of the Gods
Written by Baku Yumemakura

> *"Because it's there."*
>
> *– Mountaineer George Mallory, in an interview with* The New York Times.

In every era, adventurers seek unexplored territory. In the Age of Discovery, it was the new continent; for the Apollo Project during the Cold War, it was the surface of the moon; and for half of the twentieth century, it was the last place on Earth where no one had gone—a summit.

Mountain climbing is often used as a metaphor for our lives. We all have our own mountains—our own *it*. But reaching this point in my life, I nearly lost confidence that I knew what my *it* was.

It was then that an editor at *Da Vinci* named Yokosato suggested a book to me: the Shibata Renzaburo Award–winning mountaineering masterpiece *The Summit of the Gods* by Baku Yumemakura.

If you're feeling lost in life or are considering abandoning your climb, I recommend this novel. Forty-below temperatures, altitude sickness, strong winds, avalanches, falling rocks, frostbite, starvation, thirst—for terrestrial life-forms, no conditions are more extreme than what is in this book. The unrelenting and sadistic descriptions are so thorough and complete that the reader loses sense of where they are. Even though you know it's just a book, you will feel the coldness and suffocation until, unable to endure the pain and the shivering, you'll want to shout, "Please, make it stop!"

But the men, gazing single-mindedly up to the summit, do not throw away their dream. They choose to hold on to it and become one with the mountain. Admittedly, that may seem a selfish and foolish act, but it's impossible to avoid being overcome by the heroic will of the men who kept pursuing their dream, even paying the ultimate price. *The Summit of the Gods* spans 1,000 pages across two volumes; having scaled those two paper mountains alongside the hell-bent mountaineers, I was able to once again face my own *it*.

Summit of the Gods introduces us to two mountaineers. One is Joji Habu, a climber of legendary talent. He is a solitary man with a particular obsession with taking on unbeaten summits, seasons, routes, or restrictions on equipment. Now forty-nine, he seeks to achieve what no one else has done before—a solo winter ascent of Mount Everest's southwest face without bottled oxygen.

> *That would be merely imitating someone else's route. This is my route—the direct route, the one no one has done before. I can carve it into the face of the rock.*

My *it* is just like Habu's. He has taken what no one else has done before and made it into reality. More than that, he has intentionally chosen the dangerous, untrodden roads. That is my mountain as well.

The second protagonist and narrator of *The Mountain of the Gods* is a cameraman named Makoto Fukamachi. While in pursuit of a mystery, he tracks down Habu and is both inspired by the veteran climber and inexorably drawn to the mountain. But, lacking self-confidence, Fukamachi constantly struggles with an inferiority complex and a compulsive fear of being abandoned on the mountain. And so he decides to follow behind in Habu's footsteps. When Fukamachi continues climbing at the end, I realized that my *it* was actually his.

> *I suppose I will return alive.*
> *I suppose I will return alive, and then come back to the mountain.*
> *I suppose will go on repeating that.*
> *That is what I can do.*
> *That is all I can do.*

I had thought I was like Habu, running at the forefront, but Fukamachi's monologue—his *satori*, or awakening—jolted me. That was it. The person I am now, this older version of myself, is not Habu, but Fukamachi.

Already a quarter of a century has passed since my first *it* came to be. Looking back, it was all I had. To lose it would have been to lose myself. Even if I have to abandon everything else, I have to continue.

> *"I don't climb the mountain because it's there—I climb because I'm here. [...] That is all I am. Unlike other people, I didn't choose the mountain out of all the possible things I could do. It is all I have. That's why I do it."*

Making video games is my *it*. Just like the mountain captivated those men, video games drew me away from my previous path, saving me.

And yet, times have changed. The mountain I've climbed—the creating of video games—is undergoing a seismic shift, and its form is changing. But I suppose I will keep climbing. Not "because it's there." But rather, because it's not there.

■ JULY 2012

The Summit of the Gods

Written by Baku Yumemakura and published by Shueisha in August 2000. At the time of this writing, the novel has not been translated into English. A manga adaptation scripted by Baku Yumemakura and illustrated by Jiro Taniguchi was published in *Business Jump* magazine from 2000– 2003. The manga was translated into English by Kumar Sivasubramanian and published in five volumes by Fanfare/Ponent Mon from 2009–2015.

The heroic life of a natural-born climber for whom mountains were everything.

Mount Everest's summit—the closest point on Earth to the heavens, a challenge the men in this novel risk their lives to conquer. For those who desperately wish to see the summit of the gods with their own eyes, I recommend Jiro Taniguichi's manga adaptation. Taniguichi's detailed artwork inspires another kind of awe for the mountain. ■

MAKE THE IMPLAUSIBLE (FICTION) PLAUSIBLE (FACT)

The City & The City
by China Miéville

The City & The City is a science fiction novel that elevates a far-fetched concept.

The unidentified corpse of a murdered young woman is discovered in the fictional city-state of Besźel somewhere in the Balkans. The story follows Inspector Borlú in first person point of view as he attempts to solve the case. And right now, you might be thinking, "Oh, just another hard-boiled novel?"

But then comes page 18: *Most of those around us were in Besźel so we saw them. [...] Of the exceptions, some we realized when we glanced were elsewhere, so unsaw.* Then on page 25: *The Pont Mahest was crowded, locally and elsewhere.*

Then on page 40 comes another, more definite clue: *Sariska mocked me in my mind as I turned back to that night-lit city, and this time I looked and saw its neighbour. Illicit, but I did.*

The two countries of Besźel and Ul Qoma share the same geographical space in an adjacent and sometimes overlapping patchwork. There is no physical barrier like the Berlin Wall; the two city-states share streets and the same land. Citizens of each side can see and hear the other. But over a long history, they have been made to train themselves to see and unsee, and hear and unhear; to construct the border in their minds and act—and think—as if the other doesn't exist. Transgressing the border (breaching) is strictly forbidden, and a secretive organization (Breach) exists to prevent and contain any breaches. Fear of the organization plays a large part in the system.

Further in the story, we learn that the victim was killed "elsewhere" and brought "local." Inspector Borlú undergoes training ("acclimatization"), receives his paperwork for travel, and crosses the border into Ul Qoma. Through his continued investigation, he begins looking into the supposed existence of a third city, Orciny, located between the two. Apparently, the victim had been a PhD student in archeology and her studies into the third city had gotten her into trouble. As the story progresses, the whodunit crosshatches into a sci-fi mystery concerning the nature of the two cities.

Few novels have been able to make such an out-there idea feel real.

Many sci-fi neologisms appear in this book—*total, alter, crosshatch, protubes, breach, dissensi.* Also present are many familiar cultural artifacts from our present lives—Google, Amazon, MySpace, Harry Potter, Power Rangers.

A fundamental charm of reading fiction is experiencing a story of the possible shift gears into the impossible. But this novel takes the opposite approach; Miéville begins with an outrageously implausible story and convinces the reader to accept it as ordinary fact. Unlike the twentieth-century model of SF, which refuted fantasy and occult phenomena through scientific exploration, *The City & The City* instead successfully creates realism by carefully interweaving the ordinary. When I was in Besźel in part one, I dismissed *The City & The City* as an urban police procedural. After crossing over to Ul Qoma in part two, I discovered with surprise that *The City & The City* was an urban fantasy. In part three, standing in the Breach, recognizing *The City & The City* was urban literature, I got the chills.

Though *The City & The City* is a mystery novel, by breaching genres, it becomes something more deeply enjoyable—a crosshatch.

I am currently (in 2012) beginning preparations to open Kojima Productions Los Angeles. If the new studio gets off the ground, I will likely be traveling frequently back and forth between Tokyo and LA. The two teams may frequently breach sides. By deciding on a global goal, which side which studio is in becomes no longer relevant. The studios will exist between the city and the city.

Cities are aggregations of memes. But my studios will exist between Tokyo and LA, in a third place, as a true global studio. I don't want our memes to be just like before, only made into a patchwork with something American. I want Breach memes; global in the truest sense, sent out to protube into the world.

Inspector Borlú closes the story with this:

> *We are all philosophers here where I am, and we debate among many other things the question of where it is we live. On that issue I am a liberal. I live in the interstice, yes, but I live in both the city and the city.*

■ AUGUST 2012

The City & The City

Written by China Miéville and published by Macmillan (and Del Rey in the US) in May 2009. Translated into Japanese by Masamichi Higurashi and published by Hayakawa in December 2011.

Mystery? SF?
A crosshatch genre-breaching novel.

If cities are aggregations of memes, how would memes aggregate throughout two nations that share the same geographical space?

The City & The City leaps over the boundaries between existing genres such as science fiction and hardboiled mystery and shows off new possibilities for entertainment. *The City & The City* received high praise from Kazuo Ishiguro and swept all the major SF and fantasy awards, including the Hugo, the Clarke, and the World Fantasy Award. ■

MEMES DISCARD THEIR OLD SKINS TO BUILD A NEW FUTURE

All She Was Worth
Written by Miyuki Miyabe and translated by Alfred Birnbaum

Everything is becoming electronic. All sorts of tangible objects, capable of being said to exist in a specific location, are being taken off to some far-off place where they don't exist anywhere. These once physical objects with mass and form have all been digitized into cyberspace, no longer able to be directly touched.

Even before our digital era, one particular part of our lives was immaterialized in the name of convenience: money. In Japan, credit cards first began to be used during the period of rapid economic growth in the early 1960s, and when their usage became widespread, the abuse of credit among younger people and the resulting personal bankruptcies became a major social problem. In the 1990s, Miyuki Miyabe wrote *All She Was Worth*, a mystery novel that directly grappled with the cultural blight of spiraling debt. It is a masterpiece among masterpieces that ranks in my top fifty all-time favorite books.

> *And so the dead leave their traces in the living, much as shed clothes retain someone's body heat.*

I've long maintained that *All She Was Worth* is the Heisei era's version of *Inspector Imanishi Investigates*. Where Seicho Matsumoto's

Imanishi involves the hand of destiny guiding the path to hell, *All She Was Worth* depicts hell's chariot lurking in our everyday lives. This is a story of the traces (memes) left behind by an ordinary woman, one who struggled to find happiness and committed crimes in its pursuit. It is also a story acknowledging the memes of the harsh society she discarded. Memes will propagate; but also, much like DNA intermixing and negotiating to form genes, memes discard their old skins to build a new future.

Twenty years have passed since *All She Was Worth* was published. The changing times have shed old memes and birthed new breeding grounds of malady. As our pastimes and our daily routine have become digitized, a new spark smolders—one that could become a new infernal chariot. The recent "complete gacha" controversy over predatory practices in social games may be one warning sign—and a reason why *All She Was Worth* still resonates with the 2012 reader.

Money has lost its physical essence, and a woman becomes trapped in an ever-expanding hell of credit-card debt. She discards her past to escape that hell, while a police detective on medical leave picks up the pieces of her cast-off skin in an attempt to make her real again. The push and pull of the two sides to the story is why *All She Was Worth* remains regarded as among the best social detective novels (a subgenre that contextualizes the mystery within wider social or political issues).

But the prescient social commentary is not the only reason I love this novel most among all of Miyabe's many works. To keep on living, the unfortunate woman had no choice but to erase her past and steal another woman's life, and through the memes she left behind, I began to feel something special for her.

"Do you know why snakes shed their skin? [...] Because they believe that if they shed their skin enough times, they'll eventually grow legs."

Within the novel, the woman's words, deeds, personality, and appearance are not directly described, but instead only glimpsed through evidence such as her résumé or group photographs. We only catch brief and abstract impressions of her past through vague hearsay; her actual statements or feelings are never expressly given to us. We don't know the thoughts of the woman named Kyoko Shinjo, who has put on Shoko Sekine's past like a skin, or what led her to her crime. The most important part of a detective story—the reveal and explanation—is never realized all the way to its conclusion. But as I turned the pages, I never lost sight of her formless legs.

The ending scene is worthy of special mention. Our detective finally gets his chance to confront the criminal he's been pursuing. But the veteran policeman, who has captured many heinous criminals in his time, expresses emotions that run counter to detective-novel conventions.

In his thoughts were only questions. He felt no righteous anger. [...] This had never happened before. Not even once.

Yes. In all the mysteries I have read before this, I never felt like this at the final reveal. Not even once.

I'd feel easier if you did run away.

Yes. I feel the same as him. In all the mystery novels I have read before this, I never thought I'd feel easier if the culprit got away.

I thought that if I ever met you, I wanted to hear your story. The story no one would hear. The story you've carried alone. The months you've spent running with nowhere to go. The months you've spent living in hiding.

By holding the entrance of the woman until the very end, a woman who by all rights should not exist, Miyabe connects the story's future not to something tangible or numerical, but out beyond—to the reader.

I still can't forget the last two sentences of the last page.

There will be plenty of time, Kyoko.
    Starting from now, as Tamotsu's hand comes to rest on your shoulder.

And there I closed the book. But she is still waiting in that place, never having grown her legs, and my hand rests on her shoulder.

■ OCTOBER 2012

All She Was Worth
Written by Miyuki Miyabe and published by Futaba in July 1992. Translated into English by Alfred Birnbaum and published by Kodansha International in November 1996.

A young woman who vanished like a ghost, and the simple happiness she sought.

While on sick leave from the force, Detective Honma is asked to track down Shoko Sekine, the fiancée of a distant relative. He had discovered her previous personal bankruptcy due to ruinous credit-card debt, and when he confronted her, she disappeared. Honma attempts to find her but soon discovers she has thoroughly erased her past. What reason compelled her to do so? And, driven to desperation by debt, what has she done in order to seize a normal kind of happiness? *All She Was Worth* paints a plaintive portrait of a pitiable woman who has abandoned herself. ■

BEYOND THE PERFECT CRIME COMES A SENSE OF ACCOMPLISH- MENT, DIVORCED FROM ANY GREAT CAUSE

Shadow 81
Written by Lucien Nahum

Absolutely my all-time favorite! I've never encountered a plot that surpasses it.

In front of me I have a reprint of *Shadow 81*. I just now finished reading the novel for the first time in thirty-five years. Two years ago, I wrote the above quote for the book's *obi* for the "Hayakawa Books that made Hideo Kojima" promotion.

I encountered this outrageously plotted novel in the spring of my second year of junior high. The science fiction and foreign novels I liked to read were almost all published by Hayakawa or Sogen Mystery. But then in the bookstore one day, a faceup stack of *Shadow 81* caught my eye in the new-release section. The publisher: Shinchosha. At the time, I considered Shinchosha a stodgy company, dealing in literature and classics, so this immediately captured my interest. What was *that* publisher doing putting out foreign genre fiction? And with their usual style of a tactfully beautiful cover, no less! (When Hayakawa reprinted *Shadow 81*, they designed a new cover but stuck very close to the Shinchosha edition, only with the silhouetted airplanes flying at a level perspective rather than viewed from below.)

Shadow 81 glued me to my seat.

A 747 jumbo jet (call sign PGA 81) bound to Honolulu from LA is hijacked by a state-of-the-art TX-75E swing-wing VTOL fighter-bomber. The title of the novel references the call sign of the hijacker's plane—*Shadow 81*. Here, Lucien Nahum takes an incredible plot—so audacious that no one else would think of it, let alone write a book about it—and through the addition of an almost excessive amount of detail, creates a flawless result. The proof lies in the complete lack of likenesses or imitations before or since. This is the one and only genre novel to successfully realize a hijacking by a fighter plane.

Even when only taken as a mystery, *Shadow 81* is superb. Leading up to the final reveal of the primary culprit's identity and motive, the series of twists and misleads would belong in a Jeffery Deaver novel today. The story also offers an aspect of social satire of America's dark underside amid the Vietnam War. But despite being a story of shadows, the unique characters and witty dialogue and prose keep the mood light.

By packing in enough reality to fill a hijacking how-to manual, Nahum takes a concept so outlandish as to never be repeated and impressively elevates it to a completely plausible adventure story. Take this sequence, for example, where the hijacker dumps the traces of his crime into the sea:

> *All items now listed as unnecessary went over the side at regular intervals: table, seven reclining chairs, six air mattresses, two beach umbrellas, cooler, beer, soft drinks, and superfluous cans of food.*

The list goes so far as to include the specific amounts of each discarded object. Throughout the novel, the culprit's meticulous preparations and the careful depictions of the plot's execution are surprisingly engrossing.

When I first read *Shadow 81*, I was accustomed to reading adventure stories with heroes who were almost without exception establishment figures—policemen, soldiers, government agents, and so on. The stories all followed the implicit rule that light stands for good and darkness stands for evil, that law and order are inherently a moral good. I had kept a polite distance from noir novels that placed the lawbreakers on the side of the noble cause, as *Shadow 81* does. But *Shadow 81* is strangely refreshing; within its shadow, a bright light is visible. I don't know if that's simply because the criminals never spill a drop of blood, not even their own; or if nonviolence being an intentional stance is what matters. Unlike typical hijackings which rely on using human shields, their plot is more intellectual and mathematical—more like a con game. The ending, exhilarating and skillfully delivered, leaves feelings of satisfaction, and even the culprits' motives and beliefs stir sympathy. Beyond the perfect crime comes a sense of accomplishment, divorced from any great cause and unlike anything I'd experienced from *noir*.

Despite being a work of such high caliber, the Shinchosha edition went out of print, and *Shadow*'s memes were cut short. But then, in 2008, Hayakawa reprinted the illusive novel and brought it once again into the light of the bookstores. And I never would've dreamed it would have my quote on the *obi*!

Having been handed the baton of *Shadow*'s memes, I looked out at the new generation and didn't mince words, writing, "Absolutely my all time favorite!"

I couldn't think of anything better to say than that.

In front of me now is the fourth printing of the second edition, published by Hayakawa just this year. Next to it, I've placed a finger-marked Shinchosha first edition (reobtained used) so that I can look at them side by side.

The TX-75E (call sign Shadow 81) had been developed in secret to have the longest operating time possible for a fighter-bomber. Though it may have lost just a little altitude since the Shinchosha cover, the aircraft still flies on above my head.

■ NOVEMBER 2012

Shadow 81
Written by Lucien Nahum and published by Doubleday in 1975. Translated into Japanese by Keiji Nakano and published by Shinchosha in April 1977.

A hijacking story that changed how foreign novels were published in Japan.

A thrilling twenty-million-dollar hijacking plot runs circles around the American government and military.

Shadow 81 began the now commonplace trend of publishing translated novels straight to paperback. Though its publication broadened Japan's foreign-novel fanbase and transformed the way translated novels were published, its ideas and plot brooked no imitations. Even today, this exciting and captivating novel has not lost any of its luster. ■

OUR WORLD IS AN AGGREGATE OF MODEST STORIES (MEMES)

Metal Gear Solid: Guns of the Patriots
Written by Project Itoh and translated by Nathan A Collins

> *A great many storytellers will be coming. That's right—Hideo Kojima's enfants terribles. I am one myself. Or at least, I would like to be seen as one; to be one. So, won't you also tell your stories without fear?*
>
> —Project Itoh, *Hideo Kojima: Storyteller of Gods After the Gods Have Gone*

Satoshi Itoh was among the fans who most deeply understood my works (my memes), to the extent he became known as a "Kojima fundamentalist." After his authorial debut (under the name Project Itoh), we grew to be friends and respected each other as creators possessing similar tastes. But in the spring of 2009, with his career as an author only having just begun, Itoh passed away. Suddenly, I had lost a recipient of my memes and a precious son—an enfant terrible.

A year and a half before his death, I asked Itoh to write the novelization for *MGS4*. Not because I blithely wanted to make use of an up-and-coming writer. I wanted this young, talented novelist and fellow possessor of my memes to connect my story about memes from a video game into a different medium.

My long deliberation on the nature of novelizations produced a story informed by the meaning of telling the Metal Gear story— a story about stories, a story about what the Metal Gear saga is, what it symbolizes about the structure of the world we live in, and even an evaluation of Metal Gear.

Itoh met my every hope. He didn't merely trace along the video game's plot points and visuals. Even though the dialogue remained mostly true to the game, and aside from the final chapter, he didn't add extra scenes, the novel became a fully realized story written with an insightful, steady hand in a way that no other writer could have done. The story hadn't been novelized, it was Itoh-ized. Whether the reader has completed the game, hasn't played it yet, or is completely unfamiliar with the *MGS* series, the story will convey its memes just the same.

That is Project Itoh's *Metal Gear Solid: Guns of the Patriots*.

Still, I'm glad I met Snake. Through the days of our fight together, he taught me what it meant to be alive. And I learned that as you live, you etch your life inside other people.

I hear Itoh speaking passionately through Otacon's voice, telling us that to inherit another person's meme is part of being alive. Even after he has gone, Itoh's meme will be etched inside the hearts of his readers.

Itoh inherited my memes, but the *MGS4* he reconstructed as a storyteller is his own story too. His battle against his illness and his conceptions of *MGS4* synchronized with Otacon and Raiden, and this new story was born. Itoh explored the theme of memes through the process of communicating them, and though he hadn't been given the time to pass on his DNA, his arrangement of letters of a different sort will carry on his genetic information in perpetuity.

People live to be remembered by others, no matter in what form. People die. But death is not defeat. [...] The significance of our deeds will live on, passed like echoes from one person to the next.

Though the Satoshi Itoh of flesh and blood is no longer with us, the story of Project Itoh lives on. Just as my memes took root in him during his youth, Project Itoh's meme seeds are spreading out across the world. From them the next Project Itoh will likely be born.

This year, I will turn fifty years old. Working in the studio is fatiguing even on a physical level. Normally, this is the time I should be setting up my successor and thinking about retirement. But the person to whom I'd handed over the baton has preceded me. All I can do is pick up Itoh's last wishes (his memes). And so I will continue telling stories. Because, as Itoh wrote, our world is an aggregate of modest stories. And through his memes, Itoh showed me the importance of handing down those stories.

People never truly ceased to be. Like a river flowing through those who speak for us, human existence endured within both the physical body as well as stories passed down.

After Itoh left us, I began writing this series of articles for *Da Vinci* in search of new receivers of my memes. Much like our lives, this series will one day come to an end. But the story of My Lovable Memes and the memes I've introduced, which deserve to be loved, will continue to be passed down, as will the memes of Project Itoh.

Even though I'm part of it, I can't help but be moved by the wonder of the story that carries the meme of Satoshi Itoh becoming Hideo Kojima, and Hideo Kojima returning to Project Itoh.

■ JANUARY 2013

Metal Gear Solid: Guns of the Patriots
Written by Project Itoh and published by Kadokawa in March 2010.
Translated into English by Nathan A. Collins and published by Viz Media's
Haikasoru in June 2012.

A double helix woven from Hideo Kojima and Project Itoh's memes.

Itoh was rushed to the hospital immediately following our meeting
to plan the novelization. "I am Otacon, and I am Raiden, reconstructed and stuck in a hospital," he said, and he wrote the entire
manuscript from his bed. He made Otacon the narrator so that he
could project himself into the novel. Everything else flowed from
there. Project Itoh, the storyteller, etched himself indelibly into
this book. ■

BY LINKING OUR HEARTS AND SOULS WITH THE NEXT GENERATION, WE ARE SPARED FROM OUR BATTLE AGAINST SOLITUDE

Kamen Rider 1971 **(Color Complete Edition Box Set)**
Written and illustrated by Shotaro Ishinomori

A gigantic poster hung on the wall outside the seventh-floor art gallery of the Nihonbashi Mitsukoshi Main Store. Filling the paper from edge to edge was a lineup of all the different Kamen Riders over the history of the series. Above the Riders stood two large kanji: *Henshin!* (Transform!) Families waited in line to take cell phone pictures of themselves in front of the display, and the fathers and sons and brothers came up with their own transformation poses with the poster at their backs. Inside the gallery was the *Kamen Rider* 40th Anniversary Exhibition. There was a wide range of fans, from parents in their forties to babies still in their strollers; from Showa-era *Rider* fans to ones of the current Heisei era. When our turn came, I stood my son—who likes *Kamen Rider Wars*—in front of the poster, while I positioned myself beside the old, un-posed Kamen Rider 1, said "Transform!" and tapped the screen of my iPhone. Just then, on the phone's screen, I noticed a sentence written on the poster.

The Riders taught me about bravery and justice.

Having finished the photo session, the group squeezed into the art gallery, where the majority of the crowd divided up into smaller groups by age, because each generation has their own favorite Rider from the time of their childhood. The younger people who were unfamiliar with the original series proceeded straight ahead, while the members of the old guard, myself included, halted before the display of Shotaro Ishinomori's artist's palette directly past the entrance. The palette still carried the vibrant paint from his regular use. Without realizing it, I had let go of my son's hand as I gazed at an original manga page, in color, farther along the display. The page was from *Kamen Rider*'s time in *Weekly Bokura Magazine*. The panel layout, the composition, and the sensation of speed were just incredible. And the art was breathtakingly beautiful. Ishinomori straddled the line between manga and the more adult-oriented *gekiga*—or maybe between Japanese manga and Franco-Belgian comics. Or maybe I should say the art was just Ishinomori. By the time I came back down to reality, the Heisei-era *Rider* gang of moms and children—my son among them—had moved on to the display of *Rider* costumes from the TV show. Only my Showa generation had lingered behind to gaze in enraptured awe at the pages of Ishonomori's manga.

There, on those pages, I saw something for the first time in forty years: the scene of that first heroic transformation—a scene so glorious it became something divine. Pasted onto the paper was this line:

"I am the warrior of justice, sent by nature itself! I am **KAMEN RIDER!!"**

The manga version of *Kamen Rider* (Ishinomori drew the manga until Part 6 with Riders 1 and 2) is different from the TV version and more prominently displays Ishinomori's creative voice. The most striking difference is that, unlike the immediate transformations of the TV show, the Rider puts on his mask and suit. The mask is not, as it so commonly is in superhero stories, a tool of convenience for hiding the hero's alter ego. Kamen Rider wears his mask to hide the scars from his cyborg surgery that reappear whenever he feels rage or sorrow.

One particular scene, exclusive to the manga, leaves a powerful impression. In Part 3 ("The Revival of Cobra Man"), Takeshi Hongo, who had been made into a cyborg against his will, stands at a mirror and soliloquizes in anguish that his artificial face and body are nothing more than another mask.

> *"I am human yet not! The most tragic part is that those whom I should be able to call brother are the very monsters that I am destined to fight! I am all alone in this world...! But...even if I am alone, I... No, it's because I am alone that I must fight! I must continue to fight!! I am the only one who can stop Shocker from taking over the world!"*

He faces the solitude and struggles of a grotesque, man-made monster. From that overwhelming isolation arises a sense of purpose; the motivation of a hero who saw no other choice but to don the mask.

The manga version doesn't make heavy use of the word *justice*, instead favoring the phrase "to protect peace and nature." *Kamen Rider* borrows the "good is rewarded and evil is punished" composition, but it's also the story of the bravery within coming to the defense of peace even when no one else will.

The series is also structured so that the protagonist passes the baton on to the next generation. In the manga, the first Kamen Rider, Takeshi Hongo, falls in Part 4 (*The 13 Kamen Riders*), and

Hayato Ichimonji carries on the hero's calling as Kamen Rider 2. The first Rider's mind and soul are linked to his successor, and in that way the Riders are spared from their battle against solitude. The Riders connect forward with their successors, just as us readers are connected from parent to child.

The TV versions are strongly influenced by the state of the world, and their image of justice is a baton that has been handed down for forty years, its hue changing along with the times.

I finished looking at the original art, took the hand of my Heisei-generation son, and repeated something that Ishinomori often said, "Kamen Rider fights for humanity's future."

Kamen Rider was our generation's hero. And he is now a hero that spans both our generation and that of our children. While showing each other the differently colored batons *Kamen Rider* entrusted to us, my son and I stepped out toward the future.

■ **AUGUST 2011**

Kamen Rider 1971 (Color Complete Edition Box Set)
Written and Illustrated by Shotaro Ishinomori

A perfect reproduction of the elusive manga, which has only been published in color one other time.

The manga that made me freeze in my tracks at the *Kamen Rider* exhibition has now been reproduced in B5-paper size. Fans have been talking about the legendary color version of the manga since its previous and only publication in *Kodansha Color Comics*, and rightly so—its expressiveness is absolutely stunning. Unlike the TV show, the loneliness and strength of the monstrous man will make you reconsider what a hero is. The luxurious collector's box set contains two volumes plus a bonus book totaling 900 pages. ■

AS WE DRIFT, ALL WE CAN DO IS FIND A NEW WAY OF LIVING

The Drifting Classroom
Written and illustrated by Kazuo Umezz

> *If the desire to preserve our species is a survival instinct, then for these men, the role of their "selfish genes" had already been fulfilled. So then why risk their lives to return home? Because they are driven to leave something not just biological, but of their humanity (their memes)—to not just live, but to return to society. The life-or-death struggle, beyond the realm of instinct, to pass on their memes—that is survival in the truest sense.*

I wrote the above in my essay on Akira Yoshimura's *Hyoryu* (Castaway).

The uncertain situation we find ourselves facing in the aftermath of 3/11 has often been likened to Sakyo Komatsu's *Japan Sinks*. Except Japan has in no way sunk. Instead, Japan is adrift, alone in the world even when the world's attention is upon is. As we Japanese drift, all we can do is find a new way of living.

I would like to bring your attention to a manga that can offer us guidance: *The Drifting Classroom*, published in the early 1970s and created by the master of horror manga, Kazuo Umezz.

The protagonist is a sixth-grade elementary schoolboy named Sho Takamatsu. One morning, a series of unfortunate events culminates with an argument with his mom, and he shouts hurtfully, though without meaning it, "I'll never come back home again!" and runs out the door. At school, a terrific earthquake strikes, and the next thing anyone knows, their school has been stranded amid a desolate desert. The 862 students and teachers have been sent along with their school to an unfamiliar world in the far-flung future, where they are forced to survive without water, food, or social order. The adults, the very people the children should have been able to rely upon, are unable to endure the senselessness of their situation and begin to go insane. A female teacher has a seizure and collapses, another loses hope and attempts suicide, the lunchroom man tries to hoard all the food for himself, and a homeroom teacher begins to slaughter the other teachers and then the students. In hardly any time at all, almost all the grown-ups are dead.

The stranded young children hold on to hope for a return to their old lives, and they fight to survive. They say, *"From now on, our mantra will be 'I'm Home!' We'll say it and say it, and maybe one day it'll come true! Let's do everything we can to make our wish come true!"* But danger hounds them without mercy. Hair-raising monsters attack; disease spreads. A power struggle erupts. The students fight each other for food. Dangers come from outside the school and from within.

The artwork is intense and surprisingly realistic for a boys' manga. But *The Drifting Classroom* is more than just its horrifying depictions of monsters and of humans suffering in extreme circumstances. Umezz mercilessly kills these children in their desperate struggle to survive. And their deaths are graphic. Umezz makes skillful use of double-page spreads to control the rhythm like a horror film, and then assaults the reader with the next scare. Between everything, your hairs will be standing on end every several pages. If that weren't enough, Umezz's hand can make even the most mundane things scary, like the sand, the rain, flooding water, cliffs, underground tunnels, and even just his zoom lines. But there's something even more terrifying than the scenery, the crazed adults, the advancing grotesque monsters, and the despair that is emphasized by the black-

and-white art. It's the children, who in order to survive become more cold and more monsterlike than the adults. I still vividly remember the scene where the protagonist gets appendicitis and has his appendix cut out without anesthetic. Every time I hear the word *appendix*, I think of that surgery scene and I pray that I never get appendicitis myself. For me, that scene made a far stronger impact than the scene in *Black Hawk Down* where the soldiers attempt to pinch their wounded comrade's femoral artery with their hands.

As a child, I liked being in school in the rain. When bad weather fashioned a curtain over the school, I would get the sensation that we were cut off from the outside world. There, beneath the dim light of the fluorescent tubes, were my familiar teachers and friends. It felt like the school became a spaceship flying through the darkness. Curiously, it wasn't lonely. When typhoons came, that feeling was even stronger, and I would imagine that I was drifting along with only the kids in my same grade. We weren't to be sent out into the world the grown-ups had prepared for us; no, we children would build a world and rules of our own. I desired to grow up in that drifting, no-questions-asked environment. And so for me, *The Drifting Classroom* isn't just a manga. It's a work of children's literature about as impactful as Verne's *Two Years' Vacation* or Golding's *Lord of the Flies*. It carries a powerful message, one of drifting rather than returning alive.

The Drifting Classroom tells a story about becoming separated from the world of the here and now, from family, friends, civilization, society. I wrote previously that the homecoming is one kind of story that conveys memes. But some stories don't end with "I'm home." At the beginning of *The Drifting Classroom*, the children are motivated to survive so that they can go home. But in the end, the manga offers a different view of bravery and the future than Akira Yoshimura's *Hyoryu* (Castaway). In the last pages, the children are transcendent, and their words carry profound resonance for us after 3/11.

"We can't go back home." [...]
"We didn't ruin the world. Others did...and now we're the only humans alive!" [...]
"We are the seeds that have been scattered in the future." [...]
"This is our world!"

Perhaps the test we are faced with now—to preserve the seeds for the future—will be a new way of living (a new meme) in which we cast ourselves adrift from the previous era.

■ **SEPTEMBER 2012**

The Drifting Classroom

Written and illustrated by Kazuo Umezz and first published in Shogakukan's *Weekly Shonen Sunday* from 1972 to 1974. Translated into English by Yuji Oniki and published by VIZ Media starting in August 2006. A new definitive edition was translated by Sheldon Drzka and published in three volumes by VIZ Media starting in October 2019.

A dystopian manga containing the entirety of fear.

No one is better at expressing fear and insanity than Kazuo Umezz. It wouldn't be a stretch to say that every possible kind of fear has been put into this manga. The corpses of grade-school children are depicted like they're nothing, and every scene is extremely brutal, but *The Drifting Classroom's* unique and peculiar world is fascinating. It is complete in three books, which also include the cover pages from its first run. The crisp printing allows for a better appreciation of the artist's descriptive pen than the original edition. ■

A SPECIAL DIARY REMINDING ME OF THE IMPORTANT THINGS THAT NEVER CHANGE

Umimachi Diary
Written and illustrated by Akimi Yoshida

Whenever summer ends, and the cicadas' flurry of song goes quiet,
I think of that town by the sea.

I lived in the Tsujido area of Kanagawa Prefecture until I was about three years old. The region was so close to the ocean that all the cars rusted immediately. My family went out often—to Kamakura, Kita-Kamakura, and Enoshima, to go clam digging, to see the Great Buddha, and so on. After that, we moved to Kansai, but in 1996 I moved back to the nearby Tokyo area, and while my oldest son was still little, he and I visited those seaside towns of my memory many times. From Kamakura we took the Enoshima electric train and saw the fish at the aquarium; then we crossed to Enoshima and ate rice bowls topped with freshly caught seafood. On the slope of the hill we stuffed our cheeks with *fukashi manju* sweet buns, rode the Enoshima ESCAR (an outdoor toll escalator) to the top (what a rip-off!), walked through the botanical garden at the summit, took a ferry back from the cave side, and ended the day at a café near the train station. I had a coffee, and my son had juice, and the café was playing Southern All-Stars songs.

I wanted to see the moon in midday.

Umimachi Diary is a coming-of-age ensemble drama set in Kamakura following four sisters and their family. The events and episodes themselves are commonplace, but Akimi Yoshida uses the medium of manga to reveal what's beyond the everyday life—the more real and less polished nature of the relationships among family and friends, and of youth and romance. This is an ambitious work that seeks to encapsulate a family not through a story but as a diary.

Then, when the boyfriend of the second daughter (Yoshino) comes to Gokurakuji and sees the sisters' house, an old, large building passed down from their grandmother, he says:

"I bet it's filled with all kinds of things."

That line perfectly fits the manga itself. Under that one roof live four sisters, with their complicated family relationship and each bearing their own problems. Even as they fight with each other, they protect the memes (the home and garden) inherited from their ancestors. The depiction of their clumsy search for a way to live as the next version of their family is lively, funny, and refreshing. If Kuniko Mukoda had made manga, this would be it.

Umimachi is not like a novel or a movie, and it transcends traditional manga. At its core, a manga is a series of still images lined up in chronological order; the connected series of still images creates a flow and action, and dialogue and sound effects, presented visually, can work as an aural stimulus. But this particular manga goes further with its internal monologues and beautiful views of Kamakura. The pictures and text combine in the mind to create not just a sense of time, but a complete, three-dimensional picture of the town's smells and warmth, the characters' expressions, and even how they see the world.

In the first chapter of the first volume, there's an incredible scene where the fourth daughter (Suzu) is remembering and grieving her father, and she weeps aloud for the first time. Those three short, enthralling pages had me crying too. First is page 58, in three panels: Suzu's eyes, Suzu's face contorting, a chest-up shot of Suzu crying out. Then on page 59, another three: Suzu covers her face with her hands, her half sisters empathetically watch over her, Suzu's face in profile at the edge of the frame. And there, a poetic narration:

> *So fierce was Suzu's wail*
> *Not even the rain of cicada song could drown it out.*

Continued, on page 60:

> *How many times has she cried this summer?*
> *Here with her father beyond saving...*

The first panel is a borderless background of summer sun filtering through screen-toned leaves. A second panel, with Suzu broken down and weeping, has no background; she is completely cut off, alone. A sound effect of the cicadas' song repeats across the page in soft lettering. From the middle of the page and down come three horizontal panels in series, showing the four sisters coming together, viewed from behind, as the viewpoint pulls away. In the first panel, the oldest sister (Sachi) places her hand on Suzu's back; in the second, Sachi pulls her in closer; in the third, the second sister leans in and offers a handkerchief.

> *...And she had to face it all alone.*

Coming into this page, the three sisters from the other mother were one group, and Suzu was on her own. But amid the droning rain of the cicadas' song, one panel shows Suzu isolated, and the next long horizontal panel has the four sisters together. Suzu isn't alone anymore. They are four sisters. When I read this, I realized, *This is what panel layouts were made to do! Only Akimi Yoshida could have done it this way!* Her lyrical combination of writing and artwork and design is what elevates *Umimachi* several dimensions higher.

I want to go back to the sunlit hill road.

Kamakura: the hilly seaside town where I was raised. As my son got older, I neglected visiting. Kobe: Another sunny seaside town. Going back to my home there became too much trouble. What I have lost, and what I must not lose. What will change, and what must not change. What I've forgotten, and what I must not forget. For me, living in the big city now, *Umimachi* is a special diary to remind me of the important things that never change.

The two who can't come home, and the two who will again.

At the end of summer, I went to Hayama with my younger son. When our train passed through Kamakura, I looked out the window and saw for the first time in a while the seaside town below. There was the sea where I had played with my dad, and where my first son and I visited when he was still young. My *diary* is still there. I think I'll start it back up again when my younger son is old enough for the trips.

■ NOVEMBER 2011

Umimachi Diary

Written and illustrated by Akimi Yoshida and published in Shogakukan's *Monthly Flowers* magazine between 2006 and 2018.

A beautiful gem of a manga delicately depicting the connections between four sisters who live in Kamakura and the people around them.

Suzu is a girl in middle school who has already lost her mother, and then her father passes away too. Meanwhile, Sachi, Yoshino, and Chika are her three half sisters from another mother, whose husband had been stolen by Suzu's mother. The four sisters meet for the first time in Yamagata for their father's funeral, and they all start living together in an old family house in Kamakura. The Kamakura scenery is drawn with delicate care, and the relationships between the four sisters and the people around them blend and interweave. Every time I read it, the tenderness and melancholy fill my heart and bring me to tears. ■

ELSEWHERE ON THIS EARTH, THERE ARE OTHER PEOPLE WHO SHARE THE SAME LONELINESS

Tout Seul (Alone)
Written and illustrated by Chabouté

When I was still in school, I wrote a novel titled *Kodoku no Toh* (The Lonely Tower). It was set in the Showa era, before the bubble economy burst. A new, fully automated conglomerate complex was about to open near Osaka Station. On the night of Christmas Eve, when the media had been invited for the pre-opening, a lonely college student (our first-person narrator) is invited to the main tower, which is fully controlled by AI. By mistake, the narrator joins the party on the top floor and, without planning on it, gets blackout drunk. The next morning, he awakes and finds that he has been imprisoned alone within the tower. The elevators from the upper floors are all locked, and so are the emergency stairs. The windows are all reinforced and computer controlled; he can neither break nor open them. The phones are all disconnected. He tries many ways of escaping, even by starting a fire, but each and every attempt is thwarted by the AI. He was already alone before coming to the tower, and before long he starts to think, *Even if I escape, will anything change for me? I have water and food, and all the comfort, information, and amusements I could hope for—better than I had outside.* He stops trying to escape and instead decides to enjoy the rich solitary life the cutting-edge AI provides. One year later, he happens to look out a window and sees that something strange is happening in the outside world...

SOLITUDE n. *The state of being alone. A lonely or secluded place.*

—(from Alone's dictionary)

I was on a lunch break in December when inside a Roppongi bookstore busy with Christmas shoppers, I found a manga titled *Tout Seul* (*Alone*), a black-and-white *bande dessinée* written and illustrated by a Frenchman. I was drawn to the book, and I picked it up and opened it to the first page. The first panel shows the surface of the ocean, drawn with a line work both strong and delicate. Then, a wave rises up, and a single seabird flies closer. Having flown a great distance, the bird glides to a rest on a handrail. But then a crashing wave interrupts the creature's repose. Covered in sea spray, the bird takes to the sky once more and flies up higher. The panels seem to advance with the flapping of its wings, and the viewpoint swings around, moving to a high-up view looking down. There, a lighthouse stands alone in the ocean like the Pharos of Alexandria.

I immediately recognized it. "That's *Kodoku no Toh*!"

I snatched up the large book like it was half its size and headed to the register. I paid the cashier and hurried back to work. I ducked into a small workspace and put a "no entry" placard on the door so that no one would interfere, and I continued reading from the prologue. Then I waited until exactly the end of the workday and brought *Alone* with me to a suite that had been set up for focused planning sessions. Alone, I read it slowly the second time. Then, reflecting on what I'd read, I read it a third time. And on that third time, I cried.

I thought, "He was alone too."

This French *bande dessinée*, created by a man born in Alsace, was so strikingly similar to the novel I'd written and kept in a drawer for nearly thirty years, I had to laugh and cry at the same time. The main character, named Alone, wears solitude like a shell. But interwoven with Alone's world is another, idealized one. I carry genes that give me a tendency to seek isolation, and when I encountered the French-imported memes of *Alone*, I realized that I still had not yet taken the first step out from my tower.

> *SYNAPOMORPHY* n. biol. *A character trait shared by two or more taxonomic groups that distinguishes a species from other organisms, and is inherited through evolution (or apomorphy) from a recent common ancestor.*

With the Heisei era came new words for solitary people—*hikikomori* (a shut-in) and *NEET* (Not in Education, Employment, or Training). But feelings of isolation and being alone aren't anything extraordinary. Elsewhere on this Earth, there are other people who share the same loneliness. By meeting lonely people outside myself, I learned how to deal with my inner loneliness; not by fighting against the outside world, but by parting with the comfort of being alone.

> *IMAGINATION* n. *The ability to form a mental image of fictional or perceived objects or concepts not actually present to the senses. The ability to invent, create, or concoct.*

There are things that being alone makes you yearn for. There are things that being alone enables you to create. And when lonely people gather together, the word *solitude* disappears, and Alone's dictionary finishes its purpose.

VOYAGE n. *An adventure undertaken to put solitude behind you. The first step from the tower in which you dwell.*

Tout Seul (Alone)

Written and illustrated by Christophe Chabouté and published by Vents d'Ouest in September 2008. Translated into Japanese by Shusaku Nakazato and published by Kokusho Kankokai in December 2010. Translated into English by Ivanka Hahnenberger and published by Gallery 13 in July 2017.

Imagination flaps its wings in a way that only a bande dessinée *can achieve.*

A malformed man named Alone was born in a lighthouse surrounded by the sea and has never set foot on land. His hobby is to look through the dictionary and imagine the things he reads. In *Alone*, Chabouté evokes overwhelming loneliness through the use of only black lines and a superior artistic ability. Though the world is monochromatic, the artist's rich imagination touched my heart and made me experience the vivid colors, and even the sounds and smells, of his world. ■

MY FIRST MEMORY OF AN ELEVATOR IS IN BLACK AND WHITE

*Ascenseur pour l'échafaud (**Elevator to the Gallows**)*
Directed by Louis Malle

In 2010, I was trapped in an elevator for the first time in my life. I was in New York City for the world tour promoting the release of *Metal Gear Solid: Peace Walker*. I'd finished an autograph session at Uniqlo Soho and got in a freight elevator to head toward the next event. The doors closed, and the elevator started—then stopped. I was trapped inside along with some of my team, the Uniqlo store supervisor, the official photographers, and our security, for thirteen people in total.

As the standstill in the cramped cabin continued, even the laid-back Americans, who had at first enjoyed the unexpected accident, gradually began to display irritation. I don't know who started it, but some people began to pound on the walls and ceiling.

Somehow, we managed to open the elevator doors with our bare hands...but all that awaited us was the elevator shaft's metal wall. The elevator had stopped perfectly in the middle between two floors. The acidic smell of panic began to spread within the confined quarters.

"We're struck in this elevator!" someone shouted.

If you were in this situation, which elevator movie would come to your mind? The famous disaster film *The Towering Inferno*? The classic action film *Speed*? Or do you go to horror with *Dawn of the Dead?* You can't predict how you'll respond to a situation that you've never experienced. When it happens, your mind will cling to a news article that you read or a movie you watched that had something to do with an elevator accident, and the degree of fear you experience will depend on what mental associations you make.

Beside me, my secretary whispered, "If we don't get out of here, won't we run out of oxygen and suffocate?"

The mood suddenly changed. I wonder if she had been thinking about a movie where that happened.

As for myself, I was recalling *Elevator to the Gallows* (1957), the first feature made by the exceptionally talented French New Wave director Louis Malle. When I was a very young child, the film happened to be playing on TV, and my father made me watch it with him. The mystique and immorality of the film's world shocked me. This noir movie remained with me strongly, if mistakenly, as a trauma inflicted upon me by the people of France.

A Parisian man and woman are in love, but she is already married. To be truly together, they plot to kill her husband, the president of the same company where the man works. But after the man kills the husband in the office and stages the scene as a suicide, he becomes trapped in the building's elevator. He needs to abscond by morning for his crime to be perfect, and he desperately tries everything he can to escape; meanwhile, after his failure to show up at their rendezvous, the woman (played by Jeanne Moreau) obsessively roams the streets, searching for him in Paris's shadows, passing headlights, and drifting cigarette smoke. Her face, despondent, seems to be the only thing not black or white; she is radiant in grays. The movie's first half has barely any dialogue, while Miles Davis's improvised trumpet adds color. *Elevator* is sometimes called the start of the New Wave (*Nouvelle Vague*); no movie before had this particular kind of coolness and flair. The entrance of a second, wild couple takes the story in an unexpected direction.

Being a film noir, the movie doesn't show law enforcement's perspective. In place of norms or morality, the film holds up a different guiding compass called "Je t'aime." When I first watched *Elevator*, that part went over my head. I was still in preschool. And anyway, when was the first time I rode in an elevator? I don't have a clear memory of it. Back when I saw the movie, there weren't that many high-rises, even in the big cities, and I probably hadn't had many opportunities to ride in one. And so I'm not sure if I saw this movie before or after I'd ridden in my first real elevator for real. My first memory of one, however, is in black and white.

That was what I thought about as the New York elevator's trapped passengers were on the verge of panic. That and, *I want to get out of here quickly so that I can go watch that movie again.*

One hour later, a rescue team came and evacuated us by ladder through the top of the elevator car. We had escaped without incident. It felt like a rescue out of some movie I'd probably seen. Once safe, the exhausted and frazzled party let out a cheer in celebration. When I got back to Japan, I bought a DVD of *Elevator to the Gallows* and watched the movie for the first time in some forty years. What I saw surprised me. The movie was nothing like my earlier impressions. At the last scene, when Jeanne Moreau strongly declares, "They can't take us apart," I couldn't help but feel sympathy for her. For the first time, I realized this wasn't a film noir, but a *hymne à l'amour.* All this time, I had been trapped inside this movie. That New York freight elevator was not the first to trap me, it was this one: the *Elevator to the Gallows.*

Because chance had led me to be stuck in an elevator, I feel another one, which had ground to a halt inside my heart long ago, has begun to move again.

■ OCTOBER 2010

Ascenseur pour l'échafaud (Elevator to the Gallows)
Directed by Louis Malle

With Jeanne Moreau's powerful line: "No one can take us apart,"
Elevator to the Gallows *is a hymn to love.*

The plan was supposed to be perfect: kill his lover's husband and stage it as a suicide, then meet her at a café. But when the man returns to the crime scene to remove a piece of incriminating evidence, he becomes trapped in an elevator, and the lovers' plans go off the rails. *Elevator to the Gallows* is a landmark achievement of suspense that has left its mark in film history. A Japanese remake was produced in 2010 starring Michiko Kichise and Hiroshi Abe. ■

A TRAVERSE TO LEAD BEYOND THE TRAGEDY, FOUND AT THE END OF THE FILM

Nordwand (North Face)
Directed by Philipp Stölzl

1936—the year of the Berlin Olympics. The Nazis promise a gold medal to anyone who climbs the Eiger's as-yet unscaled north face. The move is political; the Nazis want to use their mountaineers to prove German superiority to the world.

Amid a fierce snowstorm, the climbers cling to the Eiger's north face. One shows his completely immobilized, frostbitten arm to another and says, "My arm. It's completely stiff. I can't feel anything."

This was in a trailer I happened to see at an arthouse theater in Ginza. It was 2010, and that was my first encounter with *North Face*, a movie that left a stronger impression on me than any other.

Simply put, it's an incredible film. It's a movie that feels like a movie; the kind that the commercialized industry has stopped making. The camerawork, CG, and direction are extremely restrained, offering a dispassionate depiction of mankind and nature. The twists and turns of the climbers' hopes and despair are captured with a documentarian's touch, and character drama and political messages come in and out of view. *North Face* pierced into my heart like a piton.

Another special quality of *North Face* is that the movie changes modes like the mountain changes weather. Right out of the gate, the movie indicates it's not the war movie the preview had led me to imagine. The two lead characters, Toni and Andi, decide to challenge the "murder wall" not for the Nazis, but because it's their calling. In an early scene, the two men quit the alpine infantry in order to attempt the climb. Then, without receiving any outside assistance, they assemble their homemade equipment and bicycle the entire 700 kilometers to the mountain because they couldn't put together money for train tickets. At this point, the mists of the war movie lift and reveal the mountaineering movie in its full form.

Then, as dark clouds loom over the middle act, we expect the mountaineering movie to portray the conflict between our heroes and nature's might, but instead the movie again shifts focus and becomes a critical satire of the press.

The historic ascent becomes increasingly propagandized, and a stark contrast develops between the mountaineers and the press, who are willing participants in the information war.

The journalists ride in on the Jungfrau Railway in a touristy mood, while the mountaineers had ridden by bicycle, suffering multiple flat tires on the way. They make merry in an opulent and heated hotel, while the exhausted climbers sleep in a tent and sip barley soup cooked on a camping stove. During the day, the onlookers amuse themselves by watching the climbers through telescopes on the terrace, and at night they don tuxedos and dresses and feast on full-course dinners. Meanwhile, caught in a terrible snowstorm on the north face, the adventurers desperately huddle together in their bivouac. No carabiners or climbing ropes connect the watchers and the watched.

Four days after starting their ascent, the worsening weather forces Toni and Andi to abandon their climb. As they begin their descent, the press's demeanor radically changes.

"You either need a glorious triumph or a horrible tragedy. An unspectacular retreat…is nothing more than a few lines on page three."

From this point, the satire plummets into the tragedy of a disaster movie with avalanche force.

A great number of movies have been based on true stories. But no other disaster movie is as stiflingly heavy as this. Is this really entertainment? Is it history? A nightmare? Torture? I want to look away. I want to run away. My chest feels heavy. This is painful. This is hard. This is distressing. I can't watch any more. Is this the most tragic mountain climbing disaster in the history of the Alps? And yet, I must keep watching. I have to take it in. I have to, because the disaster in this movie happened in reality. But this movie is more than just a record of a tragic event. At the end, the film has prepared a traverse for us to go beyond the tragedy.

The film opens with something Toni had said to Louise:

"When you're at the bottom at the foot of the wall...and you look up, you ask yourself: How can anyone climb that? Why would anyone even want to? But hours later when you're at the top looking down, you've forgotten everything... Except the one person you promised you would come back to."

At the end, she responds:

"One has lived if one has loved. There are times when I find this infinitely hard to believe. Most days I feel that I am alive. And that love is the reason for that."

Yes. The disaster movie that portrayed a heroic, deadly climb concludes as a movie about love. The Eiger's north face swallows everything but the onlookers, and at the very end, they leave knowing the joy of a descent, the meaning of living, and another lofty peak they witnessed at the mountain: sublime love.

■ NOVEMBER 2010

Nordwand (North Face)
Directed by Philipp Stölzl

With character drama and political messages coming in and out of view amid the twists and turns of hope and despair, North Face pierced my heart like a piton.

Summer, 1936. Young mountaineers Toni and Andi have conquered one unassailable summit after another. Despite knowing they were being used—much like the imminent Berlin Olympics—by Nazi Germany to enhance its national prestige, the adventure seekers nevertheless attempt to become the first in history to climb the Eiger's north face (nicknamed "murder wall"). Their ascent goes smoothly until the weather abruptly worsens and traps them in a desperate situation. *North Face* is based on shocking true events that occurred on the European Alps. ∎

PART TWO

THINGS I LIKED AT A CERTAIN TIME OR PLACE

First published in *papyrus* magazine between April 2007 and June 2009

GOD'S LONELY MAN

Taxi Driver
Directed by Martin Scorsese

Loneliness has followed me my whole life. Everywhere. In bars, in cars, sidewalks, stores, everywhere. There's no escape. I'm God's lonely man.

This quote comes from a monologue spoken by Travis Bickle, the taxi driver played by Robert De Niro in the 1976 film *Taxi Driver*, directed by Martin Scorsese.

I too have struggled with feelings of loneliness since I was a child; the worst were during my adolescent years. Whether it was nighttime or the middle of the day, whether I was out in the city, at school, or doing after-school clubs—I wasn't Travis, but still, I felt loneliness everywhere. It wasn't like I didn't have anybody. I had family, I had friends. I wasn't living on an uninhabited island. I was a typical boy living in a typical town in a time when social relationships weren't as superficial as they are today. And so, I did not feel like I had the physical kind of isolation, or that I was being conspicuously aloof. But inside me, the seeping sting of loneliness was always there.

The feeling didn't only come when I was alone. Even when I was having fun with my friends, it was like a switch would flip, and the loneliness would push its way to the surface: isolation within a group, isolation within a crowd. The more I surrounded myself with people, the stronger the loneliness became. For whatever reason, the pain was always strongest at the end of the year, when the city was most bustling; the loneliness inversely proportionate to solitude. I don't know how many nights I spent sleepless with worry and fretfulness, thinking, *One day this loneliness may kill me.*

And so I tended to keep to myself. Some part of me found peace in isolation. At the time, society just didn't deal with issues of human psychology. Mental health treatments for things like PTSD and manic depression weren't commonly acknowledged. Even if I had gone to someone for help, they would have dealt with it through classic literature and not clinical psychology, so I was never able to talk to anyone about my chronic loneliness.

When did it start? Just what caused me to be this way? I can't think of any absolute reason. My father's sudden death when I was in junior high might have been a factor. But I keep coming back to how I was a latchkey kid from a young age. It was the 1970s, a time of rapid economic growth, and both my parents worked. I kept my housekey dangling from a piece of yarn around my neck like a dog tag. It was annoying whenever I did a somersault on the horizontal bar, but I still wore that key 24-7.

As a latchkey kid, I don't have any memories of someone ever coming to pick me up from school. Even if it was raining, or a typhoon was coming, or I was sick or injured, I still went home by myself and unlocked the front door with the key on my neck. And when I went inside, no one was there. I was the one to unlock the door, and I was the one to turn the lights on. Starting the air conditioner or the heater was also me. An empty home is not like one where your family is gathered waiting. Sometimes, I was so lonely, I would sit at my mom's vanity and cry. Other times, I would loiter on the streets and come home late rather than face being there alone.

But eventually this lonesome latchkey kid got smarter. I learned how to improvise a pretend family gathering. As soon as I got home, I turned on every light in every room and switched on the TV at high volume— not to watch anything, but to distract from the loneliness. Even in my adulthood, I continue the habit. Whenever I check into a hotel room, whether for business or vacation, I always turn on all the lights and power on the TV. When I'm in the bath, and when I go to sleep, the TV stays on. But by suppressing my loneliness in early childhood, I may have caused it to grow stronger than it otherwise would have been.

How would I conquer this feeling of isolation? Would I be able to overcome it? In my early adulthood, I put a lot of mental and physical effort toward that goal. To keep anyone from sensing my loneliness, I kept my outward appearance as cheerful as I could. Ironically, that only further strengthened my feelings of being alone. And that was when I came across the movie *Taxi Driver*.

Immediately, I thought, *This is my movie!* The film emanated an almost viscerally painful loneliness and simmered with resentment of the world and frustration toward unfulfilled justice. Of course, at the time I was an ordinary student living in Japan. I wasn't a New York taxi driver, and I didn't pour brandy on my cereal. I didn't take my dates to a porno theater. I certainly never attempted to assassinate a presidential candidate. And yet I *was* Travis.

The story is that of Travis Bickle, a former marine and current insomniac who works nights as a New York taxi driver. As he roams the streets, we see the garbage dump of the big city through his eyes, and the young man's loneliness and rage are depicted as something pure, romantic, and sometimes violent. *Taxi Driver* is considered one of the best movies of the 1970s. It's the product of a rare gathering of talents: Paul Schrader's excellent scripting; Scorsese's documentary-like direction; passionate performances from famous actors like De Niro, Harvey Keitel, Jodie Foster, and Peter Boyle; and Bernard Herrmann's posthumous score. (Tom Scott's weeping alto sax in the main theme is ephemeral and beautiful.)

But what moved me to tears was not the story, the direction, or the actors' techniques. It was because, through experiencing Travis's loneliness secondhand, I learned that other people, somewhere out there in the world, were like me.

I'm not the only one who thinks he's alone! A man with the same kind of feelings of isolation as me is out there driving a taxi. The thought alleviated my loneliness.

After the movie was over, I bought the same military jacket as De Niro wore for his performance, put on leather boots, and went out into the city. To complete the imitation, I thrust my hands into my pockets and walked with a slouch. As I walked the streets as Travis, something seemed to have changed. It wasn't that the movie had taught me how to battle my loneliness; Travis taught me how to keep its company.

Now thirty years have passed. That loneliness that stayed with me like a sickness has vanished as if it were never there. Had it just been the same thing that every teen and young adult goes through? I think I stopped noticing the feeling so much around the birth of my first child. I started worrying less about my own solitude and more about my family and the future of the society to which they will be tied. And then, at some point, I wasn't Travis anymore. Maybe it was when I started making video games that I became completely free from that feeling. I think I became too busy to notice the loneliness. Sometimes that feels like the answer. Now my games are played by people all over the world, whose faces I've never seen and whose names I don't know. The moment I came to that realization, the demon of loneliness fell away once and for all. Loneliness is not the same as longing for company. People are destined to be born alone and to die alone, but as long as we are alive, we are connected with the world.

Every time I get into a taxi, I always look at the driver's name on their ID card. I suppose somewhere inside, I'm looking for Travis in the driver's seat, although of course, I've never seen the name Travis Bickle there in real life. In the world of the movie, he pulled fourteen-year-old Iris from the prostitution ring, but in the real world, he pulled me out from my isolation. That's why, somewhere, someday, I wish I could catch Travis's taxi, sit in the rear seat, and tell him this:

"If God made a lonely man, then God must be lonely too.
Rather than carry your loneliness, just pick up a lonely fare.
When you realize everyone is alone, you won't be anymore."

■ **APRIL 2007**

NOVELIZATIONS: MY FIRST MEETING WITH THE THIRD FORM OF EXPRESSION

Columbo: *Publish or Perish*
(Japanese title: *The Third Last Chapter*)
Written by William Link & Richard Levinson
and translated by Mitsuyoshi Nomura

A person has many kinds of encounters in life—not just with people or places, but with movies and music, books, plays, paintings, and any other form of creative output left behind by another person or another time. Since ancient times, people have received life-sustaining encouragement and stimulation from those meetings of chance and good fortune. If I were to say which particular nutrients have been my vital sustenance for the past forty-three years, they would be movies, music, and novels, in that order.

With my top nutrient—movies—my father loved them, and so by the time I started forming memories, I was already basically being force-fed them. For my second—music—the groundwork was already laid for the same reason. When you watch movies or TV, you hear music without even trying. And so, of what I consider my three primary sources of nutrition and sustenance, I had become acclimated to movies and music and began absorbing them at a very young age.

My parents were born when the Showa-era year was still counted in a single digit (1926–1935). For their generation, books were more widespread than movies or music, so everyone else in my family was a natural bookworm. Our house was practically filled with mountains of books. My dad's room, my mom's room, and my brother's room were all packed full with books of their particular taste. The overflow that couldn't fit into any of their rooms or the common-area bookcases got put up in the attic, where the literal bookworms would find them. I, on the other hand, didn't read. Even toward the end of elementary school, I still never did. The act of reading the printed word was completely absent from my daily life.

This worried my parents a lot. Every now and then, they would buy a children's book they thought I might like—*The Three Musketeers, Two Years' Vacation*—and leave it on my desk. But I never so much as looked through the pages. I'm afraid to say that my third nutrient—books—was not something I was able to ingest without actively being pressured to do so.

In 1974, I was in fifth grade. As if swept up by the continuing-education craze, I started going to an after-school tutoring school. It wasn't that I liked studying. I wasn't even planning on taking any junior high entrance exams. But once a week, I could ride on a bus and a train for nearly an hour and go on a little adventure to the next town over. I remember having fun at first, getting to see friends from another district. But before long, I would find what became the real reason I continued going to the private tutoring school.

The school was in Ikeda City, Osaka, and they had a large bookshop, which my town did not. I never intended to go inside there at first. I liked to roam the city, which was a common if dangerous pastime for a young brat looking to push his boundaries. But one day, when it started to rain, I happened to seek the warm, safe shelter of the last place a book-hating elementary schoolkid would typically go: the bookstore.

It was nearly Christmas. Just inside the entrance, a book glared at me from the new arrivals section. This fateful book was *Columbo: Publish or Perish*. The photo on the front cover had drawn my eye, along with the book's larger-than-normal-paperback size—a brand-new format—and the striking orange *obi*-like line on the cover illustration.

Columbo is a foreign TV series that took the world by storm (you may know him for saying, "My wife, she says…"). Unlike typical detective procedurals, *Columbo* is structured with the culprit's identity being known from the opening. And the criminals are all celebrities, elites in their field, or otherwise successful people. The story is told from the criminal's point of view, while a middle-aged policeman—a stand-in for the common man—stubbornly picks apart their meticulously planned perfect crimes. The show places emphasis on the breaking of alibis and battles of wits. Younger people may better understand it if I said that *Columbo* served as the model for Koki Mitani's *Furuhata Ninzaburo*.

"Publish or Perish" was the twenty-second episode of the televised series. (In the Japanese localization, the episode was titled "The Third Last Chapter.") My fated book was not the original basis for the episode, but its novelization. Novelizations (sometimes called tie-in novels) are book adaptations of a movie or a television show. They are neither the original novel nor the filmed product of one; derived from visual media, they are a third form of expression. Novelizations of anime and video games are now an active and significant genre, but in 1974, they were still in their dawn. The word *novelization* was known by few people and carried a mysterious quality, one which appealed to a grade schooler who hated books.

At the time, I still hadn't actually seen an episode of *Columbo*. I was aware of its existence, but had never been particularly interested. Nevertheless, I picked up that book with the collage of Peter Falk's weary expressions on the front. I flipped through the pages. There, printed inside the book, were black-and-white photographs from the TV show. Those blurry monochromatic pictures jolted my imagination into motion. Without so much as reading the summary, for the first time in my life I chose a book for myself out of my own interest and purchased it with my allowance. A little dismayed by my strange behavior, I started reading the book. A photograph appeared about every twenty pages. Wanting to see what picture would come next, I pushed onward. With each photograph, I was like a swimmer coming up for another breath of air. Despite not liking books, reading this one wasn't a struggle. With enough breaths, I could swim twenty-five meters. And once I could swim twenty-five, I could do fifty, or even a kilometer. And before I knew it, I was reading without thinking about the need to come up for air. Reading had become fun. I read all 261 pages in one go. I was shocked.

"What just happened? Novelizations—no, books—are *this* fun?"

From that moment I was crazy for Columbo. I belatedly started watching the TV series too.

The next thing I knew, I was regularly stopping by that bookstore on my way home from the tutors. After the lesson, I would slip away from my friends and go by myself to the bookstore on the opposite side of the train station. As I passed the time among the books, I think some part of me believed I'd made it in with the grown-ups.

I've loved bookstores as a special place ever since. They are a repository of information, and one circuit through their aisles will give me an immediate grasp of the trends in the world. I still go to a bookstore as close to every day as I possibly can—because bookstores are where I make new encounters.

Back in fifth grade, two things were always dear to my heart: bookstores and *Columbo*. Once I'd read the rest of the "second season" (of which four had been released) and the first season (eight books), I anxiously waited for the next novel to come out. They were only released at a rate of one per month. But I still went to the bookstore every week. By that point, I'm not sure which I could say I was really attending, the tutoring school or the bookstore. I certainly wasn't putting anything into my studies. Before long, I was reaching out to other mystery novels to tide me over until the new *Columbo*. I discovered Agatha Christie and Ellery Queen in that very same bookstore. These were my first true encounters with books, and they opened the door to mysteries, science fiction, adventures, and stories of every other kind.

If I hadn't gone to that tutoring school in the next town over on that day, and if my eyes hadn't stopped on the cover of *Publish or Perish*, what would have become of me? Would I still hate reading? I may have gone my whole life without ever knowing all the many people, the time periods, and the varied stories from all over the world I met through books. I may never have gotten my current job, let alone be contributing essays to a culture magazine the likes of *papyrus*.

Publish or Perish (*The Third Last Chapter*) was also a "third prologue" that introduced me to the older medium of books. Through that novelization, I learned the enjoyment of creating stories and novelizing life. Making video games, writing stories, writing a blog, and writing this essay are all novelizations of life. Casually putting the way we live into words and expressing them might be the truest novelization of life and of our current trendy way of living.

■ JUNE 2007

FILM COMMENTATORS AS EVANGELISTS

Sunday Foreign Movie Theatre 40th Anniversary: Nagaharu Yodogawa's Classic Film Comments
Nagaharu Yodogawa

"Please look forward to next week.
Sayonara, sayonara, sayonara."

For the first time in nearly ten years, Nagaharu Yodogawa's flowing, rapid-fire speech was coming from my TV speakers! As I listened to Yodogawa's nimble commentary, all the many movies he had introduced me to over the years flashed through my mind like pictures on a revolving lantern, accompanied by memories of my youth. Before I knew it, tears were welling in my eyes.

Rocky IV was being shown on TV to coincide with the theatrical release of *Rocky Balboa*, written, directed, and starring Sylvester Stallone. Nagaharu Yodogawa's original wraparound, from the movie's September 17, 1995 broadcast of *Sunday Foreign Movie Theatre*, was included—a gift, on the show's fortieth anniversary, to those of us who had watched him over the years.

The first time I saw a foreign movie wasn't in a movie theater. (Incidentally, my first Japanese movies were a double feature of *Gamera vs. Barugon* and *Daimajin*.) I was three. Back then, there weren't DVDs or video tapes, satellite or cable TV. Movies from the West came over the analog TV signal and into our tatami-matted living room, and it was all thanks to the program that started it: *Sunday Foreign Movie Theatre*.

Before and after the feature presentation of *Sunday Foreign Movie Theatre* (which aired from April 9, 1967 to February 12, 2017), Nagaharu Yodogawa delivered a short commentary, which included a plot summary and other items worthy of note. This was the first program of its kind inside Japan. Counting its first incarnation as *Saturday Foreign Movie Theatre* (which aired from October 1, 1966 to April 1, 1967), the program has run for over forty years. These days, the wraparound commentary is gone, but Akio Otsuka (also the voice actor for *Metal Gear*'s Snake) continues to introduce each movie with a rousing voice-over.

Back when we were little kids, watching foreign movies through our TV was easy for my brother and me. The dialogue was dubbed over, so we didn't have to read subtitles. But there weren't any VCRs yet. If we missed the broadcast, that was it. We had to finish eating dinner and taking our baths before the show started at nine, and we had to watch the feature with rapt attention. We couldn't pause it whenever we liked. Eating popcorn or candy was out of the question. If we needed to go to the bathroom, we had to hold it until the next commercial break. It wasn't uncommon for my brother, my dad, and me to scramble to be the first to get to the bathroom. If we missed our chance, we had to wait all the way until the next break. Sometimes, that necessitated a predetermined order and taking of turns. At the time, I didn't know that the comments before and after the movie were prerecorded. I never even suspected it. I thought it was all done live, in time with the movie's showing, and I imagined that, like us, Yodogawa was waiting for the commercial break to go and stand at the toilet.

What made me connect so strongly with movies at such a young age? When I think about it now, I suspect it was because of Yodogawa's commentaries bookending each movie. For a child who of course didn't know anything about the movie of the week, or the industry that made it, or filmmaking vocabulary, or the directors or actors—and who especially didn't know about foreign countries—the information he provided was as welcome as it was fresh.

Thanks to his explanations, I was able to digest even the challenging movies, the frightening movies, and the sophisticated movies. In a way, the information served much like the movie programs you can buy at the cinema, and at the same time, the commentator was a reassuring presence, as if he were watching the movie with me. I don't think it would be an overstatement to say that I came back to the program every week for Yodogawa's comments. I knew nothing about the movie until the program started and he gave his introduction; I kept a passive appreciation. But as I continued to watch each week, I naturally began to learn the movies by title and the actors by their faces and names. I learned to appreciate the directors' direction, to admire the composers' music, and finally, to understand the cinematographers' camerawork.

A new DVD was released in celebration of *Sunday Foreign Movie Theatre*'s fortieth anniversary: *Nagaharu Yodogawa's Classic Film Comments*. The disc contains a compilation of fifty of Yodogawa's comments, new and old, thoughtfully selected from the program's entire history. Also included as a bonus are both the oldest surviving recording (*The Big Country*, aired April 22, 1973) and what became Yodogawa's final commentary (*Last Man Standing*, aired November 15, 1998). His performance for *Last Man Standing*, delivered despite his failing health, would pull at anyone's heartstrings. But what stood out most after watching the DVD, with its 130 minutes of fifty-two commentaries, was that even without the feature films, his discussions were purely engrossing on their own.

The heyday of films on TV lasted from the latter half of the 1960s until VCRs became ascendant in the '80s. The first such program was the aforementioned *Sunday Foreign Movie Theatre* (TV Asahi). Then came *Monday Road Show* (TBS; moved to Tuesdays in 1987) hosted by another of my favorites, Masahiro Ogi. Sometime later, the two shows were joined by the actor Tadao Takashima's *Golden Foreign Movie Theatre* (Fuji TV; moved from Fridays to Saturdays in 1981 and reformatted as *Premium Saturday* in 2006) and *Wednesday Road Show* (Nippon TV; moved to Fridays in 1985) with Haruo Mizuno's catchphrase, "Oh, aren't movies really great?" and Nini Rosso's trumpet playing "Wednesday Night." And in the late '80s, the beautiful film buff Nahoko Kimura stormed onto the scene with her popular *Thursday Foreign Movie Theatre* (TV Tokyo) and her catchphrase, "Did that leave anything in your heart?"

Looking back at that period now, I realize that a movie was playing during prime-time TV nearly every day of the week—Monday, Wednesday, Thursday, Friday, Sunday. And with each showing came a commentary. It was like living in a movie theater. It would've been harder *not* to see and learn about movies.

More than that, they were all film commentators, not film critics. Even if their titles said they were critics, during those programs, they only provided a guide and analysis. They were there to shepherd us so that we the audience could enjoy those imported articles with peace of mind. In-depth reviews were not part of the package. Their comments served to help us easily understand which people from which country made the movie, and their mind-set. Every commentator took that same stance. Because of them, we were able to eat foods we'd never tasted, or that we thought we didn't like, or that we decided we wouldn't like, or that we'd never even seen before. A critic identifies the taste of the meal before you eat it. A commentator summarizes where the ingredients came from, who the chef was, and what kind of dish has been prepared. The difference is vast.

But times changed. Foreign theater programs and film commentaries are in the past. Many of the commentators have died, and in the time of DVDs, the directors, crew, and cast can speak for themselves about their work directly to the viewer through candid behind-the-scenes documentaries and audio commentaries.

It used to be that critics existed on the creators' side of the process. They simplified creative works into easily understood pieces and tossed them down to the masses. The audience heard the thoughts and impressions of these people of culture and based their own preferences upon them. And so the creators paid great attention to the reviews. The success or failure of an undertaking relied upon the critics' reviews. But that time too is in the distant past. The rise of the internet has changed the nature of criticism. Now the members of the audience can skip past the critiques and exchange their own impressions directly with one another on message boards and online communities.

If I had been born in our current era and spent my adolescence in the absence of the film evangelists, would I have taken as much interest in movies? If those programs hadn't been created with the lofty goal of introducing foreign movies to the masses in a time of scarce entertainment, and those evangelists hadn't been given a platform, I might never have connected with movies. Only because of them, beginning with Nagaharu Yodogawa, was I able to open myself to other cultures and peoples through film.

I am keenly aware that this modern era needs evangelists too. In every era there have been evangelists of the necessities of life, of culture, and of course religion. They take it upon themselves to facilitate encounters with other lands, other races, and other times. A new seed of culture won't simply take root in a new land on its own, but requires an evangelist's steadfast devotion over time.

With technological advancement and the birth of the internet, the world has connected as one. But a certain breed of evangelists— the film commentator—has vanished. In their absence, I want to become an evangelist for different eras.

Until I do, I can't let anything make me say, "Sayonara, sayonara, sanoyara."

■ AUGUST 2007

IMAGES AND PORTRAITS OF FAMILY

Bewitched, *Little House on the Prairie*, and *Shin Chan*

People are born within our smallest unit, a family, and later build a new family around themselves. Like a biological cell dividing and replenishing, one family splits and multiplies, and through each reincarnation will continue across the ages. But I don't believe the uniquely mammalian family unit merely sprang forth from nature's aim to reliably preserve our species.

My family had four people, so to me, a family is a unit of four. There were my parents (born in Showa 5 [1930]), my brother (two years older than me), and myself. My parents were both youngest children. They left their family homes and moved together from one place to another, from Tokyo westward to Kansai, until they built a house in a new development outside of Osaka in Hyogo Prefecture in 1970. My grandparents didn't live with us. By the time of my earliest memories, both my grandfathers had passed away, and we didn't see our other relatives much. I have very few memories of seeing either grandmother, either. I think that was at least partly because both sides of the family lived far away. Visits from relatives were almost nonexistent. In a way, our newly built house in newly developed, unknown land was the beginning of our new family's history—just the four of us.

Before his death, my father often said the following, as if to shake off his homesickness:

"Mom and I are starting from here. This is your family home. You can make your start here too."

This was the dream of the common people: to take out a loan to buy land and a detached house—even if only a small one—out on the edge of the city where the land was cheap. To have a yard the width of a cat's brow, with a doghouse and most usually a Shiba or some other mix of outdoor breeds (our family didn't have a dog due to my mother's asthma). The home came at a cost—the breadwinners' arduous commute to the workplaces in the city. This was the idealized image of the Showa family, and our household too was starting out in the popular mold of the time—the nuclear family.

The blueprint for a family isn't included in our DNA; it is entirely learned through observation and imitation. And so we find ourselves needing case studies, model families to be observed and followed as a guideline.

Even at a young age, I privately looked to certain families as a guide. I didn't have close contact with many in real life, but through TV and movies, I had extended, in-depth companionships with a variety of families. I could turn on our TV and look through that curved glass and into all sorts of living rooms on the other side. I peeked in on different families from all over the world and saw them just as they were.

But the families presented in most domestically produced TV shows and anime at the time were still not nuclear families, but larger multigenerational ones.

The most prominent example is the Isono/Fugato clan from the long-running anime—and still-ongoing, since 1969—*Sazae-san*. Kuniko Mukoda's live-action *Terauchi Kantaro Ikka* (1974) is another that I watched frequently as a child. Large families were very much the norm in TV and movies and had almost nothing in common with my family's circumstances. Nuclear families were the distinct minority in Japanese-produced entertainment.

And so the first family I admired in my childhood came from overseas—the Stephens family, a nuclear family from the TV series

Bewitched (1964–1972). *Bewitched* was broadcast in America and came to Japan with dubbed voices in 1966. The popular sitcom humorously portrayed the life of the charming witch Samantha and her husband, an advertising man.

As a child, the affectionate sweetness of the couple shocked me. They kissed from morning until night and repeatedly told each other "I love you" wherever they were. Their lovey-dovey way didn't change after the birth of their daughter, Tabatha, or their son, Adam. Even when Endora (Samantha's mother) and Serena (Samantha's identical cousin) took turns trying to sabotage their marriage and split them apart, the two kept on, unperturbed, their love only deepening further. With reverence I watched this witch and mortal go out on their own, with nothing to rely upon but each other's love, and build a new and unique family.

"*I* want to build that kind of family," my young self thought, despite all the kissing. "I want a lovely family like that."

When I was just a little older, I next admired the Ingalls, the traditional family in *Little House on the Prairie*, an American TV series based on Laura Ingalls Wilder's semi-autobiographical novels. In Japan, the series first aired on NHK between 1975 and 1982 and was rerun many times due to its popularity.

For one thing, the father, Charles, was unbearably cool. He was loving, diligent, and devoted. He never gave up, wasn't embarrassed about being poor, had dignity, and persisted in doing what was right. Even though he didn't have much wealth, he nonetheless adopted orphaned children and gave them a proper upbringing. His stern but magnanimous parenting style impressed me every week.

"I wish I had a dad like that," I thought. "No, I want to become a dad like that!"

I had lost my own father by then, and my family unit had shrunk to three. I was enraptured by this idealized image of a family. I probably saw some overlap there with the Kojima family having moved to a newly developed town. *Little House on the Prairie* was set in the time of the American frontier, and the Ingalls were settlers who traveled west with little but the clothes on their backs. They put down roots in an unfamiliar territory to build from scratch a new history for their family.

But so far, my two idealized images of a family were both from a foreign country. Overseas, it was a given that children would go off on their own upon reaching adulthood. Once children got a family of their own, they would leave their parents' house and become independent, both financially and physically. But for whatever reason, that modern image of a family was not portrayed in any Japanese dramas. I always felt a sense of incongruity when watching *Sazae-san* and other Japanese extended-family dramas.

But immediately after the turn of the twenty-first century, I was pleasantly surprised to find a TV family that made me think, "Now *this* is a Heisei family, not a Showa family!" At the time, I had built my own family unit of three.

The Japan-made family that delighted me was the Nohara family from *Shin Chan* (1992–). On a whim in 2001, I went to see *Crayon Shin-Chan Arashi wo Yobu Moretsu! Otona Teikoku no Gyakushu* (Crayon Shin Chan: The Fierceness That Invites the Storm! The Adult Empire Strikes Back) with my son, who was in early elementary school, and I was immediately and firmly hooked. The Nohara family consists of Shinnosuke (Shin-chan), his younger sister Himawari, his parents Hiroshi and Misae, and their dog Shiro. Most of the time, they're kind of a squabbling mess, but whenever the family is in crisis, they all band together, Shiro included, and protect each other and fight with everything they have. Shinnosuke's father, Hiroshi, is cool! His mom, Misae, is tough! Here was a new model for a family, not because of their usual words or behavior, but because of how they can spring into action in times of emergency. Their love for each other is always inspiring, but even more so in their movies. In the earlier example of a Japanese nuclear family, the Nobi family of *Doraemon*, the parents never fight for their children, not even in the movies. The family in the *Shin Chan* movies, directed by Keiichi Hara, was an entirely new kind of proposal for a family.

Heisei-era families often only had one child. The Hidco Kojima household was one of them; my family unit was three. With three, we could be like the Nobi family, but we would never be anything like the Ingalls or even the Nohara family. Although a family is not a number, the structure of a family, the influence each member has upon each other, and the total energy output is different between families of three and four. *Shin Chan* became unquestionably livelier and more interesting after Himawari was born.

Then I was blessed with a second son, and my family unit went up to four. I finally attained that nuclear family that epitomized the mid-Showa era. But for all the idealized families I'd seen in dramas and fiction, in the real world, I haven't yet become the kind of father that would make me feel satisfied with myself. I may have reached the level of the workaholic Hiroshi, but Charles remains beyond my reach. When will I be able to stop turning to these portraits of a family and make my own worthy one in reality? I want my children to not worship idols as I have, but to be able to look to our own real-life family and be inspired to dream for their futures.

As long as families are the smallest unit in our society, we need to care for those families if we ever want the world to improve. The world is an aggregation—a colony—of families.

■ OCTOBER 2007

THE PATH FROM MY FIRST LOVE, ANNE YURI

Ultraseven

I think everyone goes through an experience of having a first love. It's the first kind of romantic feelings a person experiences after being born to this life, and the first right of passage toward becoming an adult. Without that first love, I don't see how a person gets to the love of a relationship, or heartbreak, or marriage, or divorce. But what kind of feelings count as that first step?

Is it the kind of compassionate feeling two people give and receive upon understanding each other as individuals—the kind of love that simmers on and matures over a long time? Or is it the crude, self-centered yearning that stems from a hazy interest in the opposite sex? If you could call the latter, turbulent expression first love, then my first portent came when I was only four.

In the fall of 1967, I met a woman whom I will never forget for the rest of my life. Except she wasn't real. She was a fictional character on a TV show.

And that woman was Anne Yuri from *Ultraseven* (1967–1968). She was played by Yuriko Hishimi and was the only woman in the Ultra Guard.

I was born in Soshigaya-Ōkura, the sacred land of Tsuburaya Productions. I made my first newborn's cry in the Kono Medical Clinic near the train station there. Kinuta Studio (now Toho Studios), where *Godzilla* and the *Ultraman* series were filmed, was right in front of my nose. My family lived there in Soshigaya until I was two. I've heard that the studio did a lot of location filming in that area at the time. *Ultraseven*'s connection to locations nostalgic of my formative experiences, such as Soshigaya Avenue, the Kinuta Shopping District, and the Setagaya Area Gymnasium, might be the reason I'm so drawn to the series.

Ultraseven's quality was unusually high for a TV show of its type. All the things you'd expect from a sci-fi movie were present and had been done with great attention to detail—sci-fi investigations, gadgets, costumes, and even the props. *Ultraseven* exceled in every aspect, from Okinawan screenwriters Tetsuo Kinjo's and Shozo Uehara's thematic scripts, Akio Jissoji's avant-garde direction, Toru Narita's sophisticated alien and robot designs, and the world-class special effects of Tsuburaya Productions. The series was also at the leading edge of its time, with much of its worldbuilding, design concepts, and international outlook significantly overlapping with the 1970 Osaka World Expo. *Ultraseven* left me with a feeling of the future that carried forward directly to the expo's theme, "Progress and Harmony for Mankind."

Every Sunday at 7 p.m., we kaiju lovers gathered around our TVs with bated breath. Just like its predecessor *Ultraman*, *Ultraseven* began with repeated cries of "Takeda! Takeda! Takeda!" (Takeda Pharmaceutical Company was the show's sponsor). But *Ultraseven*'s style was completely different. "Invasion" is the recurring theme, and aliens take the place of kaiju for the monsters of the week. The story is set up like a mystery where the ordinary shifts into the extraordinary. Some episodes were too scary for me to finish watching, and others, without any aliens in them at all, were difficult for me to follow. The alien invasions bring along a variety of political topics, beneath which the show explores the way Japanese people lived after the war, nationalistic opposition to the Japan-US security treaty, and more. The content was much weightier and more mature than that of its predecessor, and made *Ultraman* look carefree in comparison. The invasions weren't just a matter of simple destruction and damage, but depicted cross-cultural conflict and war. *Ultraman* is a treasure that owes its existence to the heart and soul poured into it by the creators of that specific time; it could not have been made in any other era.

That said, children at the time (myself included) didn't pay attention to such complex themes. Not as we watched it in real time, at least. We were too caught up in Ultraseven, the capsule monsters, the aliens, and the Ultra Guard's tech (the Ultra Hawk, the Pointer, and the videoceiver). The Ultra Guard's launch sequences, reminiscent of *Thunderbirds* (1965–1966), remain cool to this day. But as I kept watching new episodes, I became more and more drawn to Anne. She wasn't like the other heroines I'd seen up until that point, who were only there as an afterthought. She soon took on an even greater presence within the show than either Ultraseven or the Ultra Guard. She was breezy and cute, and she sometimes showed a glimpse of a cool, sexy side. Most of all, she had a winning smile. In addition to the Ultra Guard uniform and the white coat of the medical staff, in her off hours, she also wore the latest '60s fashion, including—sometimes—swimsuits. My cheeks would burn as I was glued to the TV. Little did I know that I was experiencing my first love.

My four-year-old self realized there was something different about my feelings toward Anne around the time of the sixth episode, "Dark Zone." That's the episode with the off-course aliens from Pegassa. There's a famous still photograph of the Alien Pegassa. Anne is sitting at her mirror brushing her hair. Behind her stands the alien, about to pounce. Anne is unaware. That situation never actually happens in the show. The photograph was only taken to be used as promotional material, but kaiju encyclopedias and magazines made frequent use of the photo.

When I looked at the photo, part of me was shouting, "Anne! Watch out! There's an alien behind you!" But another, unexplainable emotion was beginning to emerge. Whenever I looked at the photo, my face turned red. At the time, I didn't understand why. Looking back now, I think that maybe that was the first moment I recognized a woman as a woman. From that point on, every time I saw her on the show, my body would heat up. I think that was my first love, the starting point of every kind of love that came after.

The emotion revealed itself most obviously during, ironically, the final episode: "The Biggest Invasion in History: Part Two." My tears came unbidden and wouldn't stop. Watching Dan (a.k.a. Ultraseven) leaving Earth was sad, and I felt like I was losing something with the show ending, but the pain of knowing I wouldn't see Anne again was clearly stronger.

In the 1970s, Hishimi moved on from *Ultraseven* and became a sex symbol thanks to movies like *Bohachi Bushido: Code of the Forgotten Eight* (1973) and TV's *Playgirl* (also 1973). Needless to say, an Anne fan who was a young child had no means of following Hishimi's leap. I bought the 2005 DVD release of *Bohachi Bushido* but have never finished it. The movie itself is fine, but I just can't confront watching her boldly bare herself like that. In my mind, Yuriko Hishimi is Anne. Maybe I just didn't want to destroy the image of her I built up as a child with a crush.

Then I came to a turning point. In 1997, the thirtieth anniversary of *Ultraseven*, a collection of essays and photographs titled *A Letter to Anne* was published. And there, I finally was able to look at Hishimi, buxom and tastefully nude. And I had a realization:

"Hishimi will always be Anne. And Anne is Hishimi. My first love was Anne the character on the show *and* Yuriko Hishimi the real person."

As I kept reading *A Letter to Anne*, my childish emotions melted away. Printed in the book were bare, impassioned love letters to Anne from various figures in the entertainment industry. The young boys who loved her are all over Japan. We're all still devoted to her. From that point on, I began to say this when asked in interviews: "My first love was Anne."

A friend of mine, Kenji Kamiyama, directed an episode in an anthology film called *Shin Onna Tachiguishi Retsuden*. But in the movie's opening episode, "Kingyo-hime: Bekkoame no Yuri" ("Princess Goldfish: Yuri of the Tortoiseshell Candy"), directed by Mamoru Oshii, Yuriko Hishimi played her first motion picture role in 32 years. The premiere was going to be in Roppongi, and Hishimi herself was going to speak! "I have to go see it!" I thought. "I can't not go!"

I sent Kamiyama an email pleading with him to introduce me to Anne at the event.

On the day of the premiere, Oshii stood at the stage and bashfully confessed through his megaphone, "I had a crush on Anne." His impassioned words made me feel an inexplicable rush of emotions. I probably should have needed to tell her in my own words, but I felt like Oshii was speaking for me by proxy, and I was oddly relieved. I'm sorry to say that I did not get to speak to her backstage like I had hoped, but after forty years I did get to meet my first love—not as a fictional character, but as a real woman. The first woman I loved really did exist. Yuriko Hishimi hadn't changed; she was still lovely Anne. Her charming smile was alive and well.

On this fall day, on the occasion of *Ultraseven*'s fortieth anniversary and the beginning of a new series, *Ultraseven X*, at the age of forty-four, I'm writing a letter to Anne, filled with my gratitude—a love letter I should have mailed forty years ago.

As I look back on the path I've taken from my first love, there at the starting point is still Anne.

■ **DECEMBER 2007**

漫画! マンガ! MANGA! (MANGA! MANGA! MANGA!) THE STORY OF ONE DAY'S NIGHT

2001 Nights
Written and illustrated by Yukinobu Hoshino

In front of you is a Japanese keyboard. I want you to type in the characters for "manga" and have the computer convert it into a word. What kind of writing results on your screen? Is it "漫画" in kanji? Is it "マンガ" in katakana? Or is it "MANGA" in the English alphabet? Spoken aloud, manga is simply manga, but when you see the word put into kanji, katakana, or the alphabet, the difference in connotation should be surprising.

It may be hard to imagine now, but "漫画" of a long time ago conveyed no sense of time. Prewar "漫画" were primarily political cartoons and consisted of either one or four panels. The modern presentation of a series of panels in chronological succession didn't come in until after the war. Consequently, prewar "漫画" didn't have a narrative. The addition of story came with the arrival of the fore-father of modern manga, Osamu Tezuka.

Before long, "マンガ" gained broad appeal due to its diverse creative voices and depictions of society. In hardly any time at all, the medium grew a more robust subculture around it than that of the novel. Other subgenres, including boys' manga (少年マンガ), adult-targeted *gekiga* (劇画), and girls' manga (少女漫画) converged into an even broader "マンガ" culture and then went out into the world at large. Having crossed the seas and been favorably received there, "マンガ" made the next leap into "MANGA."

Thinking back to my childhood, I hardly ever read the weekly manga magazines. I remember buying monthly magazines like *Bokura* and *Boken'o*, which had comparatively higher paper quality and a greater number of color pages, but I almost never purchased any of the weeklies. I hated that distinctly cheap paper of the weekly rags. They were made to be read and thrown away, which is probably why the publishers employed recycled paper, but as a child I just didn't like how the paper looked and felt. I especially loathed the red, green, orange, or yellow tints of the paper. Even more offensive were the repulsive, battered, discolored, and finger-smudged magazines left sitting out at the barber or in an eatery or a hospital waiting room. And so I did my best to avoid reading the manga serialized in those magazines until I could buy the book versions that came out several months later. Those single-volume editions (*tankobon*) were designed for permanent collection; each contained a group of weekly chapters that had been put together all in one place, revised, and neatly bound—those were what "マンガ" were to me. And that preference hasn't changed even as I've reached upper-middle age.

My first manga—or at least the earliest I remember—would probably have to be *Tiger Mask* or *Ashita no Joe* (Tomorrow's Joe), two sports manga created by Ikki Kajiwara. When I was in preschool, everyone was crazy about them. Then, in elementary school, the influence of action-oriented *tokusatsu* TV shows naturally shifted my interest to superhero stories. Among them, I was most into Shotaro Ishinomori's (at the time he wrote under the name Ishimori) *Cyborg 009* and *Kamen Rider*. For a while, I was also crazy about the madcap comedy *The Genius Bakabon* (which had its fortieth anniversary in 2007); even after all this time, I can still draw Bakabon's dad with my eyes closed. In junior high, *Space Battleship Yamato* led me to Leiji Matsumoto; I was proud of my collection of complete sets of his works, including *Galaxy Express 999* and *Otoko Oidon*. I feel like I drew nothing but Maetel from *Galaxy Express 999* in the margins of my textbooks and notes. In senior high, I got into the Western-influenced art of Buichi Terasawa (*Cobra*). I traced over Cobra on the cover so much that the sides of the *tankobon* turned black from the graphite that rubbed off from my pencil. In college my tastes turned more mature, and I became a big fan of Katsuhiro Otomo, Ryohei Saigan, Hisashi Sakaguchi, and Shuho Itahashi.

After I graduated from college, I took a job in the video games industry. By summer, I'd had enough of the grueling commute and rented a room in Kobe's Okamoto neighborhood. It was my first time living alone. Naturally, I ate out for all three meals of the day. Every day I went to a different *katsudon* joint or casual restaurant or somewhere like that. That was the lifestyle. To my chagrin, I even started reading those weekly manga magazines I had instinctively loathed. This time, it wasn't the boys' weeklies, but ones for an older audience, such as *Big Comic*. As I shoveled down my rice-bowl meals, I discovered new talented manga creators, including Naoki Urasawa and Kenshi Hirokane. Then my bachelor's lifestyle led me to encounter another gifted creator.

I had brought only three things with me from home when I moved into my room in Okamoto: my bed, my stereo, and my bicycle (a refrigerator and washing machine were provided). I didn't even own a TV yet, and on the infrequent occasions I got back to my room early, listening to music through my headphones was the only way I could kill time. The loneliness, which I felt more keenly than most people, would keep me from sleeping, and night after night I slipped outside and went on walks. That first summer, I didn't have an air conditioner, and sometimes my room was just too hot for me to bear. My room was in a high-rise apartment building situated between Hankyu Okamoto Station and JR Settsu-Motoyama (at the time, JR was still Japanese National Railways).

Almost by miracle, several bookstores on both the Okamoto and Settsu-Motoyama sides stayed open uncommonly late. Rather than loiter in convenience stores, I was drawn to the bookstores like a summer insect to a light bulb. That was when and where I came across a manga I will remember as long as I live.

I was standing at the shelves of a small bookstore to try to distract myself from the loneliness when my eyes landed on the title of a "マンガ" that reminded me of a movie I loved. On that sleepless midsummer night, I took the "マンガ" from the shelf and flipped through the pages of Yukinobu Hoshino's *2001 Nights*.

I was shocked to discover that *2001 Nights* wasn't just manga but a work of hard SF undoubtedly made for adults. I was surprised not just because of its many beautiful artistic qualities, like the intricate artwork, distinctive design sense, and filmic layout, but also because of the serious, novel-like content. *2001 Nights* has Asimov's scientific pursuit, Clarke's lyricism, Heinlein's heroism, and even Bradbury's fantasy.

I had no idea any "マンガ" was like this. This discovery rekindled the waning fire of my sci-fi soul.

I began reading all of Hoshino's manga I could get my hands on. Back then, there weren't internet auction sites; I searched from one used bookstore or *otaku* shop to another.

Hoshino's manga are works of entertainment, but also of art and philosophy. His platform moved from a weekly magazine with a circulation in the millions to a minor monthly magazine, but he still kept on with his lofty serialized stories. When I discovered him, Hoshino's noble artistic posture deeply impressed me. I might have seen myself in him; at the time, in the shadow of the Famicom boom, I was putting together video games for a minor platform.

Japanese manga didn't spread worldwide as "MANGA" solely because of commercially popular strips driven by the editorial departments' leadership. The international success of manga is unquestionably because of the steady work of creators who stood apart from the mainstream, such as Yukinobu Hoshino and Daijiro Morohoshi (ironically, both received *Shonen Jump*'s Tezuka Award).

Nowadays, "MANGA" and video games are often given as the primary examples of Japan's cultural exports. Manga realized a great leap, going from "漫画" to "マンガ" to "MANGA" with a hop, step, and jump. On the other hand, "computer games" came to Japan and became "TV games," which then spread back out into the world following the video game crash of 1983 (known as the "Atari shock" in Japan). But video games have retained the same native meanings inside Japan and around the world.

Why won't Japanese-made games make that same leap that "MANGA" has? I think it's because video games are still a product where the market takes first priority. "マンガ" broke through the discriminatory boundary of being only for children, and some have reached the level of fine art or philosophy. Hoshino and his peers made unique works of art that could only be expressed through the medium of "MANGA," and not as novels or movies. That is what makes their works world-class, and worthy of the name "MANGA."

Kobunsha has released Hoshino's *2001 Nights* in an oversized format. If you haven't read *2001 Nights*, I hope that you will pick it up. I want you to experience firsthand that manga books aren't just for consumption. Some will remain in your heart, and some you will want to treasure for the rest of your life.

This new edition has reunited me with *2001 Nights* for the first time in twenty years. Incredibly, the manga once again filled me with limitless courage, just as it had on that summer night. Against all odds, made with only paper and pen, the story (broken up into only twenty nights) surpassed that giant of cinema *2001: A Space Odyssey* and forged a new path beyond the accepted ways of the manga industry. And though I think his work went unrecognized for too long, Hoshino broke the bindings of Japanese culture and pushed "マンガ" to the next level: "MANGA." I can only admire such a stunning achievement.

At this moment, my fingers are on a computer keyboard. I'm going to type in "geimu" and try to decide how I want the computer to convert it. Will it be a positive "芸夢" (artful dream), or a negative "迎無" (receive nothing)? Or will it remain as it always has: "ゲーム" (video game)?

I think my sleepless nights have a ways to go.

■ FEBRUARY 2008

DO THE MASSES DREAM OF *BLARUN*?

Blade Runner
Directed by Ridley Scott

> "*...a mess...gruesome...crammed to the gills with much more information than it can hold.*"
>
> – The New York Times

> "Blade Runner *is like science fiction pornography — all sensation and no heart.*"
>
> – The State and The Colombia Record

These are just two selections from critics' reactions of a certain movie that came out nearly thirty years ago. Just what kind of movie do you think would receive such scathing denunciation? Having only read those quotes, I think anyone would be curious to find out. But hearing the title would likely change that curiosity into indignation.

That maligned movie is in fact a monumental science fiction film that grew a passionate, international cult fan base and has been a great influence on later filmmakers. That movie is *Blade Runner*, and I love it. *Blade Runner* is and always has been in my top ten favorite movies of all time. I believe, as many other creators do, that if I hadn't encountered this movie, I would not be who I am today. Not a dream and not just fiction, *Blade Runner* realized a vision of the future steeped in realism.

Today people all over the world hold *Blade Runner* in high regard, but surprisingly few are aware of the movie's ignoble public reception at the time of its release. I don't just mean the reaction of the critics, either; the general moviegoers of the time preferred lighter, heartwarming entertainment and spurned the melancholic, hard-to-understand *Blade Runner*. As a result, the movie was a flop, unable to make back even half its production budget at the box office. It was too radical, too philosophical, and too ahead of its time for the masses. The movie's poor response in America was repeated in Japan when it opened there one week later. It was gone from the theaters almost as soon as it came. Far too few people in my circles went to see the movie, and without the internet, I had no opportunity to share in my excitement for *Blade Runner*. But once videotapes became widespread, the movie took on a special status, different from that of space opera SF like *Star Wars* and *Star Trek*. Those who liked it were completely enamored. It was a movie that chose its audience; an early example of a cult movie. At some point, the fans in Japan had begun to affectionately call *Blade Runner* "*BlaRun.*"

BlaRun opened in the summer of 1982—during my first year at college—with little fanfare or notice. I watched *BlaRun* by myself in a conspicuously empty auditorium of a movie theater in Osaka's Umeda district. Like many who had been able to see *BlaRun* in the theaters, the movie knocked me flat for a good while. Watching it gave me goosebumps, less from the story or themes as much as the sense of being in the future. *BlaRun*'s world was a chaotic hodgepodge, and yet it wasn't unpleasant. It didn't have the typical presence of decay or decadence that is so common in near-future SF. Also absent was the loneliness characteristic to noir. Somehow, *BlaRun*'s world teemed with a sense of vitality. In the city and the vehicles, people's fashion, billboards, and even accessories, technology became design in ways that made sense and didn't feel out of place, and that fit together remarkably well. Here cultures crossed not only the boundaries of region or nation, but of time. Brought together in one place, they coexisted with a beautiful harmony. Even the darker moments confronting life and death seemed to shimmer. *I want to live in that kind of city. I want to live in that kind of future. In that kind of world, I could live!* The last movie to make me feel such awe from its world, rather than its characters, was *2001: A Space Odyssey.* For me, the alternate world constructed by *BlaRun* was new but also nostalgic.

In 2007, an ultimate special DVD set was released in celebration of *BlaRun*'s twenty-fifth anniversary, along with various merchandise timed with the DVD release. I made a personal *BlaRun* festival out of the occasion: I bought the five-DVD set, a three-CD anniversary soundtrack, a making-of book that had been revised to include the material from the final cut, and to top it off, I reread the novel upon which the movie had been based: Philip K. Dick's *Do Androids Dream of Electric Sheep?*

A theatrical run of *Blade Runner: The Final Cut* also accompanied the DVD release. In Japan, the only showings were in Osaka's Umeda Burg 7 and Tokyo's Shinjuku Wald 9 cinemas. I had only seen *BlaRun* in the theater once during its first release, and again in a double feature with *Terminator* in Kyoto some years later, and I knew that this time might truly be my final chance to experience the movie on the big screen. As I was still in the thick of making *MGS4*, going to see the movie ought to have been out of the question, but I made the time anyway and went to the Wald 9 in Shinjuku.

The Wald 9 is a multiplex with (as the name suggests) nine small auditoriums playing various movies that change throughout the day. There is one ticket booth. Just to see what would happen, I went up and said, "One ticket for *BlaRun*, please," to the young woman working at the booth.

She said, "Huh?"

I guess the nickname isn't that well known among younger women. I pointed at theater five on the schedule and repeated, "One ticket for *BlaRun*, please," and this time she understood. I took the ticket, regathered my spirits, and headed to theater five.

The auditorium was filled with other *BlaRun* fans in their thirties and forties. Some were salarymen on their way home from work, and others had the distinctive look of people who work in the industry. Some were middle-aged men who haven't yet been able to break free of *otaku*-dom. When the movie first came out, all these types of men had been in their teens or twenties. Now they were in their prime of life and exhibiting an air of the dignity of their years and presence in society. I saw some younger women, though not many, who had been brought by the aforementioned members of the *BlaRun* generation without knowing the movie themselves. For some reason, no one was talking. No coughing or clearing of throats, either. Even the couples were silent. A peculiar tension filled the space, unlike anything I've experienced before any other showing. Everyone quietly held their gaze ahead upon movie screen, where nothing was yet being projected. It was the kind of stillness that settles over an audience in the moments before a short-distance sprint or an F1 race. And then the final cut, and *BlaRun*'s final screening, began.

When the title logo came up, the audience collectively let out their breath. Amid the pleasantly tense mood, the 117 minutes were over in an instant.

Deckard picked up the unicorn from the floor, and the elevator doors closed. The credits floated by atop Vangelis's song, and the screening was over.

My chest was tight with emotion. Roy Batty's last line echoed in my mind. The final showing had ended, but inside my heart it was still playing. When the lights came back on, the audience headed for the doors in silence. No one clapped and no one cheered. I felt a little let down. I had rarely experienced such a quiet exit. But there was nothing else to do but join their silent stream out the doors. Exiting the auditorium, I turned toward the elevator and froze. People had filled the elevator. The moviegoers were eagerly conversing. I kept hearing the word *BlaRun*. And then I understood: they weren't waiting for the elevator. The theater hadn't sold a program for the movie, but lobby cards for the final cut had been put up on display in the elevator hall, and the people there were looking at them like art in a museum. Not one person went into the elevator. Each in their own way, they were ruminating over the movie. They all loved *BlaRun*!

Never in my life had I ever been surrounded by so many *BlaRun* fans. Though I didn't know anyone's name, I spent a blissful time with those fans. *BlaRun* has several different versions, but honestly, any of them would have been fine. I'm not all that interested in un-released footage or digital retouching. I'd seen everything on video or DVD until I couldn't watch them anymore. But the truly special part of this experience was to have been able to share *BlaRun* in a theater, in this time, with other people who appreciate it. Twenty-five years ago, I wouldn't have believed it possible. It was an emotional experience, and for me, that was the real *final cut*.

I exited the theater building into a light rain, a fall shower that still carried a lingering warmth. The high-rises towered through the rain's haze. Below them, neon signs flickered in a variety of colors and languages. In the distance I heard sirens, words in other languages, and curses. Young people ate junk food on bicycles and shouted as they crossed the street. I took a step forward and onto the roadside. There before me was not Shinjuku, but Los Angeles in 2019, as dreamed up by Philip K. Dick and Ridley Scott twenty-five years ago.

I looked up at the sky and took in a deep breath. I smelled *BlaRun* in the air. I lifted my hand and touched the city. I felt *BlaRun* on my skin. I stepped into a rain puddle. I felt *BlaRun*'s warmth.

Are we still dreaming?

■ APRIL 2008

YAMATO AND A PIECE OF *ROMAN*

Space Battleship Yamato (also known as *Star Blazers*)

I became enamored with the word *roman* (like "romanticism," particularly the aspects of emotional aspiration for heroism, adventure, and lofty idealism) because of an anime every Japanese person knows: *Space Battleship Yamato* (1974–1975).

Although it's unbecoming of a man my age, I'm drawn to the words *dream* and *roman*. Of course, dreams and *roman* don't exist in any concrete form. They don't exist as material objects in the physical world. They can be pursued but never obtained. No one has ever seen their true form, and their truth will not be learned from a dictionary, even with the latest revisions. Like all the many gods mankind has created, they are an idea formed to give people a future to live for. And yet I still pursue those nebulous dreams and *roman*. Even if we never reach them, the goal is what keeps us alive. Dreams. *Roman.* A man's pride, or "a man's *roman.*"

I became enamored with the word *roman* because of an anime every Japanese person knows: *Space Battleship Yamato*. First a TV series and then a movie, *Yamato* was a revolutionary work that transformed Japanese animation and created an unprecedented "Yamato boom," a movement from which came anime merchandizing and *otaku* culture. Without *Yamato* I doubt there would have been the Japanimation that drew the world's attention, and maybe no anime business capable of providing a living. Many current creators might not be active today, myself included.

I can't think back to how I found *Yamato* without bringing back memories of my father. He was born in Showa 5 (1930). He had survived the devastating fires of the Great Tokyo Air Raid and experienced the loss of the war. The end of the war saved him from being conscripted into service, but as a boy, he had wanted to join the navy. He had an unequaled taste for alcohol, and he was also skilled with his hands, and so he liked to build plastic model battleships alongside his drink. The bathroom dry dock where we kept our bath toys contained many wrecked Yamato battleships.

One day, our dad saw the word *Yamato* on the TV listings.

"Hideo," he said. "A show about the battleship *Yamato* is going to start. I want you to watch it!"

He changed the channel on us. He was an intimidating parent, and defiance wasn't an option. And so, on October 6, 1974, when I was in fifth grade, I saw the first broadcast of *Yamato* almost by miracle.

But to an elementary student, the first episode was much too boring. Only at the very end did the anime show just a glimpse of the silhouette of battleship *Yamato*. The majestic flying spaceship of the title was nowhere to be found. And so from the next week on, I sneakily set the channel to *Saru no Gundan* (Army of the Apes). I wonder how many other living rooms had a similar story. *Saru no Gundan* and *Heidi, Girl of the Alps* steadily ate away at *Yamato*'s viewership, and eventually the anime's run ended at twenty-six episodes, rather than the initially planned thirty-nine. With that, Yamato completely vanished from my mind.

But *Yamato* didn't remain sunk. Reruns gave the show a chance to resurface. Our family had gotten into the habit of watching Yomiuri TV's anime reruns at dinnertime. Just as I had become completely sick of the incessant reruns of *Samurai Giants*, *Yamato* came back and got another chance.

Going forward, I watched *Yamato* on rerun many times. I never got tired of it. The more times I saw *Yamato*, the more I appreciated it. Soon, some of my classmates were taking pictures of the TV screen with a camera or recording the audio on a tape recorder. Slowly but surely, everyone around me came down with *Yamato* fever. Three years after its TV run, *Yamato* was made into a movie and achieved its big breakthrough.

My father passed away too soon, in the summer of 1977. (The first screening of the *Yamato* movie was in Tokyo, on August 7, the day of my father's funeral.) *Yamato*'s release was the one piece of good news that came amid the hopelessness of the loss of our family's central pillar. I had been staying at home in mourning but went with my mom to Umeda to submit the related necessary paperwork, and on the way home I bought a presale movie ticket that came with a poster. At home, I put the poster up on my bedroom wall and often looked at Starsha's face. But I couldn't mope forever. I was only an eighth-grade boy, but I was going to need *roman* to get me through to the next day, and I needed to find it before the new school trimester started.

I'll never forget the day *Yamato* opened in Kansai. I jumped onto the first train of the morning and went by myself to the Toei Palace cinemas in Umeda-Shinmichi. It was summer break. As I emerged from the Umeda subway stairs into the late-summer heat, I immediately noticed something was odd. Winding endlessly along the sidewalks and roads was a line longer than any I'd ever seen. The movie theater was far enough away I had to squint to see it. Just locating the end of the line was a trial. Word from the theater made its way from the front of the line like a game of telephone: in order to handle the crowd—including those who had been waiting overnight—showings would begin early in the morning and continue throughout the rest of the day. No one would be turned away. In the end, I wasn't able to get one of the production cels that had been rumored to be given out first come, first served, but that didn't matter. I had been able to *feel* the *Yamato* phenomenon in flesh and blood. I was not alone in its vortex. I waited for hours under the blazing sun, until finally—probably the third showing of the day—I watched *Yamato* in a fetid, packed auditorium. There, I reunited with Captain Okita, Susumu Kodai, Yuki Mori, Desler, and all the other characters. And for the first time after my father's passing, I was able to process the death of the man who loved the *Yamato*.

But just what is *Yamato*'s appeal? If I had to answer in one word, I think it would be *roman*. The total blackness of space. A single ship sails through the unknown with mankind's survival on the line. It's an unfathomable 14,800 light-year journey to Iscandar, a planet no human has ever seen. And the crew doesn't just have to get there, they have to come back with the Cosmo-Cleaner D to rid Earth of its radiation. Amid all these uncertainties, they have a one-year time limit before humanity's extinction. The crew carries a heavy duty for the survivors they leave behind on Earth. The stakes could not be higher. *Yamato* is a story about keeping a promise and about daring adventure through the vastness of space, and through both is a sense of *roman* that is becoming more and more rare in recent years.

Yamato is from a time when mankind sought *roman*, and when *roman* was more valuable than gold. Similarly popular anime like *Mobile Suit Gundam* and *Neon Genesis Evangelion* don't share the same men's *roman*, because the people who made them are of a different generation with different sensibilities. The people who survived the war and the postwar period were antiwar, yet irrationally they admired military weapons, and they carried the legacy of *roman* and of war through the lens of bushido. All these aspects are *Yamato*. These were men who were there at the start of the war and at its end; they crawled from the burning ruins into fast economic growth, and they held on strongly to the vestiges of the war and carried them inside. *Yamato* may have been one way for the parents who lived through the defeat of war to pass on the story of the Yamato to their children.

Yamato's theme songs (for the opening and ending credits) make heavy use of the word *roman*.

> "*We are the fighting men entrusted with the duty to save the Earth, and our* roman *burns strong.*"
> "*The men embarking on a journey want a piece of* roman *in their heart.*"

"The voyaging men want roman *to always remain in their sight."*

The lyrics were written by Showa-era lyricist Yu Aku. You can see in the lyrics that *roman* is always paired with "man" or "men." The song evokes the feelings of the men of the sea, and of Showa *roman* remarkably well.

In 2008, a limited-edition DVD box set of *Yamato*'s TV version was released from a new HD remaster in commemoration of its thirtieth anniversary. A 1/700 scale plastic model kit of the *Yamato* was included. I want to take this opportunity to savor *Yamato* one more time.

Lately, kids and adults alike have stopped dreaming. They don't feel *roman* anymore. But that is not necessarily a cause to worry; dreams and *roman* haven't always been a part of our ecosystem since ancient times. To the contrary, dreams and *roman* obstruct reality. And with the rise of that thinking, dreams and *roman*, whether in fiction or our daily lives, became locked away behind the pretext that they were unrealistic. Dreams and *roman* are in the process of becoming tacitly obsolete in our modern society.

And yet I wonder. Is it better to completely let go of the unattainable—of that untainted greed that lets us believe in tomorrow even when we're at rock bottom? When we challenge what we believe to be impossible, is that not when we feel *roman*?

Dreams and *roman* have not been easily attained in any era. They are like the sun looked up at from the ground. Have we not pursued them even when we knew we could never reach them? It is those who wholeheartedly chase *roman* that can carry it inside them.

Whenever I feel like I'm about to lose sight of my dreams or *roman*, or when I feel like I'm about to give up on them, I sing to myself the verse of the scarlet scarf in *Yamato*'s ending song. And when I do, I see the Yamato sailing off into that great black sea, and I fill with the kind of bravery we know as *roman*.

The scarlet scarf
the girl was waving
Who was she waving it for?
Couldn't it be for anyone?
Let each believe it was for him
The men embarking on a journey
want a piece of roman *in their heart.*

(Lyrics: Yu Aku; Composer: Hiroshi Miyagawa)

■ **JUNE** 2008

JOY DIVISION
AND THOSE DAYS
(THESE DAYS)

Joy Division

Walk in silence
Don't walk away, in silence

See the danger, always danger
Endless talking, life rebuilding
Don't walk away

Walk in silence
Don't turn away, in silence

Your confusion, my illusion
Worn like a mask of self-hate, confronts and then dies
Don't walk away

People like you find it easy
Naked to see, walking on air
Hunting by the rivers, through the streets, every corner
Abandoned too soon, set down with due care

Don't walk away, in silence
Don't walk away

—Joy Division, "Atmosphere"

May 18 is a date that holds a special meaning for me. May 18 is the anniversary of the death of Ian Curtis, the vocalist for the legendary cult band from Manchester, Joy Division. In 1980, on the eve of their first US/Canada tour, Ian Curtis ended his own life. He was only twenty-three.

Whenever someone asks me my favorite band, I answer without fail: Joy Division. And if they ask me which is the most important album, I respond without hesitation: their second album, *Closer*. To me, Joy Division is more than simply a band or its music. I'd almost say we share a common soul, but at the least I've been deeply influenced by them—by their music, their lyrics, their visual style, their approach toward living, their spirit, and even their views on life and death. Even though Ian is gone and his band is no more, that has never changed. When life is hard, when I feel like I'm losing sight of myself, when work has me feeling down, I always listen to Joy Division. But even in the middle of a bright and sunny day, I periodically listen to Ian's voice and his band's pulse and melody—not because they will cheer me up like another band might, and not because their nimble rhythm will shake my body and release my stress, but because by intoxicating myself in their sublime and perilously melancholy world, I reaffirm my own place. Joy Division is my bedrock, sharing in my dread of loneliness and death and the consequent feelings of depression. I am like a believer going to church every Sunday to listen to the sermon; a bookworm reading his favorite book again and again until the pages wear out; an art collector looking at his favorite painting every morning. I don't get excited or emboldened. I don't laugh, cry, or feel moved. Joy Division is an empty space, forever tranquil. The act of returning to that space is what Joy Division is to me.

Having lost their vocalist—the face of their band—the remaining members changed their name to New Order and admirably overcame the tragedy. Somewhat ironically, their song "Blue Monday," written about Ian's death, became their breakthrough hit. Then, as everyone knows, New Order found terrific success and forever cemented their status as a major, world-class band, and they continue to be active to this day.

Regrettably, I didn't start listening to Joy Division until some time after Ian was gone. I first learned about them from the Japanese liner notes (written by Michinari Yamada) to the first album by Tears for Fears. The liner notes contained this sentence: "Inspiration for their current sound came from Joy Division, a band fronted by Ian Curtis, active around the beginning of the 1980s and legendary among fans of their kind of music." I think I read those comments around 1983, the same time New Order's "Blue Monday" became a big hit in Japan, and so I learned about New Order at about the same time as Joy Division. I'm not sure which was first. But due to the success of "Blue Monday," Joy Division's albums received a belated Japanese release. My LPs and twelve-inch singles are Japanese editions, and I probably bought them around that time. Curiously, I was getting deep into Joy Division, but I wasn't that interested in New Order, even though they were taking the world by storm at the time. I wouldn't start liking New Order themselves until their album *Low Life*, which came out a couple years later in 1985.

My college years were a particularly dark time in my life. I wasn't able to let go of my dream of making movies, but neither could I find my break. The days went by with nothing but languor and anguish. My college life was so lacking in vitality I might have been dead. I had no one to go to for advice, and not even anyone to just talk to. That was when I met Ian of Joy Division, and Etsuko Takano, the writer of *Nijussai no Genten* (my starting point at age twenty). Neither were alive. Both had taken their own lives while still young. Rather than the hopeless loneliness I felt inside crowds of the living, I chose to converse with the dead, whom I could never reach. Rather than the living people who would not understand me, I chose the dead who shared the same understanding as me. During my time with Joy Division, I conversed with the distant dead and through doing so managed to hang on to life. Joy Division was my silent confidant; Joy Division saved my life. That is why they are so special to me.

Twenty-five years later, Joy Division once again returned to popularity thanks to the movie *Control*, the first feature film from Dutch photographer Anton Corbijn. *Control* is a biographical movie, filmed in black and white, following the life of Ian Curtis from his late teens until his suicide. It is a movie about Ian Curtis, but it is also about Joy Division. With *Control*'s theatrical debut, Joy Division was suddenly out in the public. As a longtime fan, I was thrilled, but it was also a busy time to be one. I bought *Control*'s soundtrack. And Paul Smith *Control* T-shirts. And Anton Corbijn's limited-edition photo book, *In Control*. And Katja Ruge's photo book, *Fotoreportage23: In Search of Ian Curtis*. I also read the autobiography written by Ian's wife, Deborah, *Touching from a Distance*, which I had acquired previously. I also bought the digitally remastered collector's editions of their albums *Unknown Pleasures* and *Closer* and the rarities compilation *Still*. I also took the opportunity to add to my collection the two-disc compilation *The Best of Joy Division*. By miracle, and through connections within Konami's London branch, I managed to secure the UK exclusives *Joy Division: Martin Hannett's Personal Mixes* and *Joy Division: Let the Movie Begin*.

Walking through Shibuya, I saw *Control* posters. The CD shop was playing Joy Division. The bookstore had put together a Joy Division display. The movie theater was running trailers for Joy Division–related material. Joy Division was everywhere in the city. It was a Joy Division festival. As a fan, I had never dreamed such a fortuitous day would come. I hope that many people, particularly the younger generations, will hear their music because of it. I want people to know about the band that we lost. I want them to experience the sensitive man who left us during his youth.

Capping off the festival was a documentary movie, *Joy Division*, directed by Grant Gee and timed to release on the anniversary of Ian's death.

Through my experience of this festival, including the documentary film, an old question has resurfaced in my thoughts. Should we die young and go on forever? Or should we live long and, even if we make for a disgraceful sight doing it, show the world we continue to fight? Which makes the true legend? Which is the real hero? In the documentary, the members of New Order give interviews as living witnesses. They are wealthy now, but also physically old and mentally fatigued. The film ends with the surviving members playing a Joy Division song, intercut with them and Ian back when he was still alive. What might have seemed a simple comparison of past and present, or the change from Joy Division to New Order was, to a fan, heartbreaking to see. To go on performing into one's older years, is that legendary? As I watched the end of the documentary, a strange feeling came over me. Was Ian's death—and the death of Joy Division—the source of their appeal?

In those days when Joy Division first came into my life, I was a lonely young man at his closest approach to death. I stayed in this world, and all of a sudden I'm about to turn forty-five (as of 2008). Though I may make for a disgraceful sight, I keep on living, and I keep on fighting. Maybe that was the only path for the band members who had lost Ian, and the others around him, and those of us who were strongly impacted by his death. And yet, I'm not sure. Die and stop time, or live and be eroded by it? I still don't know the answer. That's why I've kept on listening to Joy Division for twenty-five years.

Someday I hope to visit Ian Curtis's grave in Macclesfield. His gravestone is inscribed with the title of what has been called Joy Division's greatest song:

Ian Curtis
18–5–80
Love Will Tear Us Apart

■ AUGUST 2008

KOSAKU SHIMA AND OUR FATHERS' JOB TITLES

Shacho Shima Kosaku (President Kosaku Shima)
Written and illustrated by Kenshi Hirokane

The other day, a press conference was held at Shinagawa's Stellar Ball to announce the appointment of a new president at a major electronics company. The event has been widely reported, not just on internet news sites but as a top story in newspapers and TV. But why is everyone making such a fuss?

The company in the national limelight is Hatsushiba Goyo Holdings. Does that ring a bell?

Hatsushiba Goyo Holdings is a newly formed holding company that was created when Hatsushiba Electronics acquired Goyo Electronics in order to merge their business. Now that I've said Hatsushiba Electronics, some of you probably got it. That's right, the company where *that* man works—the man who was picked to be the president of the new holding company. He is Japan's most famous salaryman, the hero to all fathers and salarymen, Kosaku Shima (age sixty). Even those who don't usually read manga should have at least heard of his name.

Kosaku Shima is the protagonist of a manga series written and illustrated by Kenshi Hirokane that began its run in 1983 under the title *Section Chief Kosaku Shima*. Over the past 25 years, Kosaku Shima has charged his way up the corporate ladder, advancing from *Section Chief*, to *Division Chief*, to *Managing Director*, to *Executive Managing Director*, to *Senior Managing Director*, and now, finally, he has reached the top: *President*! Of course, Kosaku Shima is a fictional character. But his presence in our culture is strong enough to warrant coverage in real-life news. Kosaku Shima is a rarity for a manga character; he is nationally famous, he is regarded as a hero, and (unlike Sazae-san) he ages in real time. I have lived through the same times as him and added the same share of years to my age, and the news of his success delighted and thrilled me beyond words.

Kosaku Shima was born into the baby boom generation, graduated from Waseda University, and got a job with a large corporation called Hatsushiba Electronics. He is a completely average salaryman with few defining traits, except that he always solves crises at the last moment, has highly capable superiors and subordinates, and brings difficult projects to successful results. And, almost by miracle, he keeps moving up. This isn't the American dream—this is the salaryman dream. And now, this past May, he attained the pinnacle of salaryman achievement, the title of president and CEO. *Kosaku Shima* offers a salaryman fantasy in a time when the reality for such men is ruthless and cruel.

On the other hand, the story of competition for advancement within a top-tier corporation might not resonate that well with a younger reader. "Graduate from a top university, get permanent employment with a top company, work like hell, and try to get ahead" was the previous generation's way—or rather, that of their fathers' generation; something long gone. In truth, that part bothered me too, and I never read *Section Chief Kosaku Shima* when the manga first ran.

I was born in 1963, considerably later than the baby boom. But I was told as a child to "graduate from a top university, get permanent employment with a top company" as if that was the greatest good. Back then we didn't even have the words *NEET* (a person not in education, employment or training) or *freeter* (a person subsisting only on part-time work). We were taught that society revolved around your academic history and job title.

My father was a chemist involved in the development of new medicines, but within the corporate structure, he was another salaryman. He was jostled about in the trains, he had conflicts with his coworkers, he complained about his fatigue but kept on working, and he finally managed to get a house of his own, in a Kansai suburb newly carved out from the mountains. I grew up there starting in the latter part of elementary school. And in that town too, the same slogan reigned. The town had no past, and so a way was needed to scrutinize the class and identity of all these outsiders. The answer: academic background and job title. In this hodgepodge of a town with no history to speak of, we transplants had nothing else to cling to. Upon meeting new people, children and parents alike competed against each other through their current or future academic history and job titles. It was like the card game War.

"I am a such-and-such at such-and-such company."

"I want to study such-and-such at such-and-such University."

And so I rebelled. I chose a different world: an industry where titles weren't necessary, and a new profession where all that mattered was a person's ability—the video game business. As a result, in the 1980s, a manga titled *Section Chief Kosaku Shima* didn't interest me at all. It wasn't that I hated Hirokane's work, either. I had lovingly read every volume of his *Human Crossing* as well as the science fiction of his early career, and I considered myself a Hirokane fan.

So then what made me start reading *Kosaku Shima*? My work environment completely changed. In 1993, seven years after joining Konami, I was put in charge of a small team—Development Group 5, with not even ten people and few sales. I was promoted to associate general manager. I was still only thirty. In addition to developing video games, I had new responsibilities as a manager in an organization—dealing with personnel, administration, budgeting, and more. I had experience as a game designer, but none as an associate general manager. I was doing everything for the first time. It was then I once again came across *Section Chief Kosaku Shima* in the bookstore. Our job titles weren't exactly the same, but associate general manager and section chief were functionally similar in scale. *Section Chief Kosaku Shima* was there to alleviate the troubles

I couldn't tell anyone and the worries I didn't want anyone to sense in me. Caught between the organization and the work, the new Associate General Manager Hideo Kojima was all alone in his fight—except for the shadow support of Section Chief Kosaku Shima.

That isn't the full extent of our story. While Kosaku Shima was still section chief, I was promoted to general manager of a production division, and then he became general manager of advertising. In 1996, my division split off as a subsidiary of Konami and I became the new company's vice president and member of the board of directors, and he returned to his parent company and was promoted to *Managing Director Kosaku Shima*. Then he became *Senior Managing Director Kosaku Shima*, and I returned to my parent company and became a corporate officer. Looking back on it now, it almost seems like Kosaku Shima and I were competing in real time to see who could get the next promotion first. Those coincidences give Kosaku Shima a special place in my heart.

The title of the *Kosaku Shima* series always leads with his current position, but the story is *not* about his title. If anything, I would call *Kosaku Shima* a drama about personal growth across a lifetime of battles, and how the man faced them, with each job title representing his many battlefields (his station and surrounding environment). Because his titles feature so prominently at the beginning of the manga's name, *Kosaku Shima* will always be perceived as a story of career advancement and success, but when I think back on the series, I realize that he had always valued himself over a title when choosing his job.

When the character was still young, Kosaku Shima said something I'll never forget. It was when he was section chief. I have no doubt that at the time, neither the character nor his creator, Kenshi Hirokane, had yet dreamed that he would one day rise to become the president of the company.

"I would rather work like a dog in a job I like than to be promoted in a job I hate."
—*from "Step 59: Everything Must Change"*

In the business world—and this goes not just in Japan but overseas as well—people often exchange business cards when they first meet. Within this exchange is an implicit establishment of mutual trust with their respective job titles acting as a credit line that can be drawn upon.

"I am so-and-so, general manager at this-or-that company." "I am so-and-so, president of this-or-that, a major firm."

Sometimes, it can feel as if first impressions and business negotiations are all decided by the title written on a person's business card. But is that really true? Job titles don't hire people. Job titles don't make anything. Job titles don't create profits. A job title alone doesn't give a person charisma. Only a person's specific talents and charm, commensurate to the position, give meaning to the title written on the card. When Kosaku Shima was a section chief, he was different from other section chiefs. The people in his story don't respect the section chief, they respect Kosaku Shima the section chief. We don't all love *a* section chief, we love Section Chief Kosaku Shima.

Though I am a game designer, I also am a corporate businessman. Promotions and changes of department come with the territory. Now I am an executive and I take part in business operations, while, like Kosaku Shima, I am also a salaryman of a past generation. Nevertheless, I want to keep on going as I have up until now, not as a man burdened with his title, but as a game designer. Titles are meaningless. Titles don't bring acclaim. Titles don't stay behind. Titles are transient. They are circumstantial and have no worth on their own. What people respond to and appreciate are not the organizations or their official positions.

What a working man requires, more than any title, is his own identity. His own way of living. His own judgment. His own name, given to him by his parents. And the value that name currently holds.

On the left-hand side of my business card (as of 2008) this is printed:

Creative Officer, Konami Digital Entertainment
Director, Kojima Productions
Hideo Kojima

But I want to be remembered for what I've done, not for any title I've held. I want to use what's left of my life for the sake of my personal mission, not my position.

And so when I exchange business cards, I introduce myself by saying:

"I am Hideo Kojima, game designer."

■ OCTOBER 2008

THE STAR
CHILDREN
OF 2011

2001: A Space Odyssey
Directed by Stanley Kubrick

oes anything perfect exist in our imperfect world? What if I restricted the question to exclude anything created by nature, and include only that which has been made by man? If any of humanity, flung out by the Creator by chance, managed to themselves create something perfect, shouldn't those creators be praised as a type of transcendent being? Looking back on my forty-five years of life (as of 2008), I have only encountered a limited number of perfect works. If I had to name just one, it would be Stanley Kubrick's *2001: A Space Odyssey*. Released in 1968, *2001* is a monumental science fiction movie known to practically everyone. *2001* is my all-time number-one favorite movie, which I will forever revere. Up until now I've consciously avoided speaking publicly about the film because to me *2001* is that immense and that personal. But if anyone is unfortunate enough to have still not seen it yet, I truly hope that they will. To go on living one's days without knowing this movie is like closing the door to one's own evolution and future.

I first heard about *2001* in 1978, exactly ten years after its first theatrical run. I was in my third year of junior high. *Star Wars* had become a blockbuster success in America the year before, but because distribution delays pushed the Japanese theatrical release until the following year, the resulting unprecedented SF craze arrived in Japan ahead of the film that sparked it. Suffering from *Star Wars* withdrawal, SF fanatics had no choice but to seek out other movies instead, including *Message from Space* (which reached the big screen in Japan *before* the movie it ripped off) and Spielberg's *Close Encounters of the Third Kind*. TV networks made special SF programming blocks, and books covered SF movies past and present. I think that was where I found it—a mook (a cross between a magazine and a book) titled *Space SF Movie Book: Encounters with the Unknown—Star Wars and 2001: A Space Odyssey*. Reeled in by the articles on *Star Wars*, I bought the book on reflex. The same book also contained a special feature on *2001*.

■ The Dawn of Man

The mook's *2001* feature contained real meat: full-color artwork and stills, an illustrated diagram of the spacecraft, interviews with Osamu Tezuka and Kubrick (by film critic Masahiro Ogi, conducted over the phone), and an essay by SF writer and translator Tetsu Yano. That was my first contact with *2001*, and it left a terrific impression. I loved reading hard SF and hoped to one day become an astronaut; it was only natural that I would be more drawn to the sensibilities of *2001* than those of the space opera *Star Wars*. But my wishes of seeing *2001* in the theater went unanswered. Beyond its initial run and a second run the following year, there had been no plans for a rerelease. I had to make do with reading Arthur C. Clarke's original novel (sadly, he passed away in March 2008) and listening to a radio-play adaptation. Then, the same year *Star Wars* came to Japan, *2001* finally received a theatrical rerelease. I think I saw it at Osaka's OS Cinerama. I was lucky that my first experience of watching *2001* was in Cinerama. From that point on, whenever *2001* got another rerelease, I went to see it on the big screen.

■ Jupiter Mission

For me, *2001* is not merely a movie; it's an experience. I had no religion; but in this movie, I met space, I met a new concept of God, and I met the god of artistic creation. I trembled in amazement and intellectual excitement. No matter where I looked on the screen, I couldn't believe that what I was seeing had been made by the hand of man. It was abstract but scientific; abstruse, but simple; everything is perfect, therefore everything is incomplete; a movie, but not a movie. It was something that transcended film. Was this really something man-made? How did anyone make this, especially *when* they made it? I would go back to watch *2001* again as many times as opportunity allowed. I was like the anthropoids in the movie, touching that silent monolith and seeking its knowledge. But I still haven't received an answer. I don't think I ever will find one. And yet I still want to seek it. I want to go on the odyssey again. And *2001 was* an odyssey, something that used the medium of the movie screen in an entirely new way.

Because *2001* is such a perfect movie, I endeavor to view it in only the perfect environment. Of course, I've seen it a few times on TV or videocassette, but that has only confirmed my belief that this movie should be experienced on a gigantic screen. The odyssey can only be fully enjoyed on the scale of a 70 millimeter or Cinema-Scope projection. And so, despite being a fan, I never bought *2001* on videotape, laserdisc, or DVD. This wasn't just because the image quality was inferior. *2001* is a god among movies, and I didn't want to presume to do anything like pause, fast forward, or rewind based on my own convenience.

But then, this summer, I saw that Warner Bros. had released a two-disc special edition as part of their Platinum Collection, and I finally bought a copy. And this being *2001*, once I bought my own copy, I couldn't help but watch the making-of and listen to the audio commentary. This was a mistake. In the making-of documentary, various people who worked on the movie gave their personal answers and opinions and revealed how they made the movie. I don't need their interpretation of the story. I don't need to hear them talk about what difficulties they experienced. I have no need for a talking monolith. Since then, the DVD case has remained closed.

▪ Intermission

2001 is in no way a movie of the past. On the contrary, it was ahead of its time. After the end of the Cold War, humanity stepped back from space development, and we still haven't completed an orbital station or a lunar base. We haven't developed an interplanetary spacecraft like the *Discovery*, cryogenic hibernation systems for the journey, or an AI that has emotions like HAL 9000. The themes and worldview expressed through the movie have not dulled in the forty years since the film's release, and all the digital technology and VFX available today couldn't recreate the same degree of filmmaking perfection.

In the summer of 2008, Ginza's Togeki Cinema exhibited the 2001 restoration of *2001* for about three weeks. 2008 marks exactly forty years since the film's release (the American theatrical release was April 6, 1968, and the Japanese theatrical release was April 11, 1968), and apparently would have been Kubrick's eightieth birthday. I finally managed to get away to see one of the last screenings on July 16.

2001 still moves me no matter how many times I see it. I was elated to be able to see the movie one more time on a big screen, and I thanked the manager of the Togeki along with the space god that must be out there. Watching the film again, I noticed something: to those of us who make a living through artistic creation, *2001* is our monolith. Clarke said in an interview somewhere that his first conception of the monolith was not a stone slab but a screen that would display various instructional images, like how to make tools. In other words, in the initial concept the monolith *was* movies.

Two ideas presented by the movie, briefly stated, are that from the perspective of humanity, aliens of higher intelligence would be to us transcendent beings no different from gods, and that these godlike entities are surely somewhere out in space watching over us. But to me, *2001* itself is the symbol of a greatly advanced civilization. When I think of the movie, all I see is a monolith. Forty years since its first release, the times have radically changed. We are now in the twenty-first century, a time of widespread environmental destruction and terrorism. Kubrick's prediction—that the Cold War would propel us to expand into space—was in a sense far off the mark. But even with all our advances in semiconductors and miniaturization, which Kubrick did not foresee, no one has made a single movie so perfect as to surpass this one.

■ Jupiter and Beyond the Infinite

Any story tied down to a specific year is going to become obsolete the moment time overtakes it. Much like computer games, anything that uses advanced technology as a selling point—SF or otherwise—is born with the sad fate that its expiration date will become suspect even before its sell-by date arrives. In my teens, I loved science fiction. Like a child anxiously looking toward his next birthday, I was always aware of when the dates mentioned in SF works were coming in real life. In the late '70s, I measured the next nearest future as 1984, from George Orwell's *1984*. When that year arrived, what had been a dream was now a thing belonging to the past, and I would need a new year to mark the future. Coming into the '90s, I moved the future to 1997, from John Carpenter's *Escape from New York* (titled *New York 1997* in Japan). Then reality overtook fiction once more, and the dream became a skeleton of history. With the twenty-first century's footsteps drawing near, my next checkpoint was also the last remaining measure I had on hand: 2001. Then 2001 came. But I realized something in that moment. *2001* was different from other works of science fiction. Although we had crossed into the number the year in its title, the film belongs as much to the future as it ever has.

My internal clock has stopped at 2001, and there it will stay until the times—and I—truly reach *2001*. When our world has caught up with the perfection that is that film, and we creators manage to surpass it, that clock will return to motion. When that time comes, we will have finished our odyssey to Jupiter, and maybe a new, infinite odyssey will commence, just as Dave is reborn into a star child when he touches the monolith at the end of the film.

The monolith remains standing before us, placed in our path by a god named Kubrick.

■ **DECEMBER** 2008

THE GENIUS BAKABON: "IT'LL BE FINE!"

Tensai Bakabon (*The Genius Bakabon*)
Written and illustrated by Fujio Akatsuka

When I was a child, whenever anyone asked me, "Where does the sun rise?" I would always sing to myself a particular verse from a song.

> *The sun rises from the west*
> *And sets in the east. (Oh, dear!)*
> *It'll be fine.*
> *It'll be fine.*
> *Bon-Bon-Bakabon*
> *Bakabon-Bon*
> *A family of geniuses, Bakabon-Bon*

I'm sure many people remember those lines from the opening song to the popular anime *The Genius Bakabon* (the first series ran from September 25, 1971 to June 24, 1972).

Of course, the song is wrong. On this Earth, the sun rises from the east and sets in the west, and as long as our planet's rotation doesn't somehow reverse, the opposite will never be true. Everyone should have learned that fact in science class, if nowhere else. If I had written an answer as wrong as that on a test, I'm sure I would've been called straight to the teacher's office. But still, whenever I needed to think about which way the sun rises, I always sang that verse from memory. And it was all because I liked the powerful statement in the chorus: "It'll be fine!" To say nothing of our solar system, the sun symbolizes the center of our physical world; its existence is absolute. Well, why *shouldn't* it rise from the opposite way? Don't worry about it. It'll be fine! The lyrics present a bald-faced error, and then affirm it. To me, this rebellious spirit made the song sound like an upbeat kind of rock music.

When children are being taught which hand is their right hand, they are told, "The hand you hold chopsticks with is your right hand." That explanation is repeated again and again, like a magic incantation, until it has been memorized by reflex in mind and body. That's how *The Genius Bakabon*'s theme song was for me. I memorized which way the sun rises and sets by thinking of the lyrics (the sun rises in the west and sets in the east) and answering in the opposite. But the song meant more to me than that. Later on in life, I realized it presented, in condensed form, the same philosophy and approach toward life as those of the series' creator, Fujio Akatsuka.

If I were to name the manga creators who have most influenced me throughout my life, they would be Shotaro Ishinomori and *Bakabon*'s Fujio Akatsuka. Ishinomori taught me about masculine bravery, and Akatsuka taught me comedy. If anyone was my comedy mentor, regardless of medium, it could only be that genius. I don't mean to suggest that I haven't been influenced by any others, such as Chaplin and Peter Sellers, and TV acts like the Drifters, Shochiku Shinkigeki, and Yoshimoto Shinkigeki. But the foundation of my humor is without question Fujio Akatsuka's madcap gag comedy. For me, I think what set him apart as something special is that his comedy was in a medium completely different from movies, TV, or the stage. Unlike sitcoms, a manga isn't staged to get an entire audience to laugh all together. Whenever I'm feeling down, I can turn the pages for myself and laugh at my own pace. I don't deny the value in being part of a crowd and laughing so hard my sides hurt, but sometimes I need a more introspective kind of comedy to heal life's wounds. And that is what Akatsuka's manga is to me—a source of smaller laughter to lead to tomorrow and to affirm the feeling that I am alive.

I think my first encounter with Akatsuka was through the TV anime adaptation of *Osomatsu-kun*. But despite *Osomatsu-kun* being the home of beloved characters like Iyami (known for his catchphrase exclamation "Sheeh!") and Chibita, for whatever reason—maybe because I was still very young—it was *Moretsu Ataro* that fundamentally drew me to Akatsuka's world. When I was little, my forehead was more prominent than those of most other kids, and my family called me "Dekoppachi" after Ataro's younger brother with a huge forehead. I didn't like it, but I didn't hate it either; after all, *Ataro* was an extremely popular manga and had been made into an anime. That was probably when it started. Before I knew it, I was drawing Nyarome, Kemunpasu, Beshi, and other *Ataro* characters everywhere and anywhere I could. Akatsuka designed his characters as simple, fun caricatures that could be easily drawn by children. At the time, even kids with no artistic ability could at least make a Kemunpasu. Then, after I started going to elementary school, I came across *The Genius Bakabon*. Even though I hated the weekly manga magazines, I still bought the *Weekly Shonen Magazine* for *Bakabon*. And as I mentioned above, the TV anime was undeniably a major influence. I think it was around third grade when I got really into *Bakabon*. I drew Bakabon's dad at every opportunity—in my notebooks, textbooks, on drawing paper, in my diary, on desks and on walls at school. I even became able to properly draw the differences between the dad's face in profile and from the front, something that was said to be a challenge even for Akatsuka's assistants. Eventually, I could draw him with my eyes closed. I still feel the same way drawing him to this day. In fact, when signing autograph boards, I've drawn Bakabon's dad in the corner on more than a few occasions. In any case, I think I've drawn that character more times in my life than any other.

Curiously, very few proper nouns appeared in *Bakabon*'s world (this is characteristic of Akatsuka's works). Almost no characters have names, either. Bakabon's dad. Bakabon's mom. The policeman with connected eyes. The old man who says "rerere." No one has an actual name, just an identifier based on their job or role, or maybe a nickname at most. That's different from *Sazae-san*. Bakabon's dad doesn't have a defined job. He never does anything related to having a job. He might be unemployed (he is a gardener in the anime, among other things, depending on the version). How he financially supports his family remains a mystery. The main character, Bakabon, is never shown attending elementary school. We have no idea what his grades are. His friends never show up in the story either. That's different from *Doraemon*. Bakabon isn't *Sazae-san*'s Katsuo or *Doraemon*'s Nobita. *The Genius Bakabon* doesn't take place within the societal constructs of the workplace or school. It's a story of nobody. The setting is undefined. In each chapter, the story happens either in Bakabon's house or on an unnamed street. The stories take place in completely unremarkable routine daily life. In this structureless, uninhibited world, *Bakabon* depicts a surrealistic extraordinary version of the ordinary. Everyone is a fool and a genius. *Bakabon* is an alternate reality where these outsiders are so unsophisticated and unbound by rules that they seem stunningly brilliant. It is an outlandish manga, entirely divorced from traditional Japanese ideas of identity rooted in name, pedigree, academic background, and social status.

I'm certain that *The Genius Bakabon* had a major impact on me. *Bakabon* presented countless bits of nonsense that the common sense of the time wasn't equipped to handle and countless turns of phrase I'd never heard in movies or novels. *Bakabon* had an avant-garde point of view and an unconventional mindset that no formal education would provide. For me, Akatsuka's manga was not nonsense; it was a *new* sense. From that point on, I wanted to be an idiot and a genius.

Sadly, Fujio Akatsuka passed away on August 2, 2008, at the age of seventy-two. First was Shotaro Ishinomori; now another of my heroes has gone. But the absurdist gag humor he created has undoubtedly been passed forward into the future. And now, in a time when our future is potentially darker than ever, his humor will be needed.

After Akatsuka's death, many of his books and manga got new printings, and new collections and mooks were published. There was also a TV special titled, *It'll Be Fine! The Legendary Fujio Akatsuka*. I suspect the occasion led a great many people to realize the innumerable amount of works and famous phrases he left behind. I suspect we all reaffirmed the influence that his works had on our upbringing. I also suspect we all rediscovered that we were each one of his creations, one of his children, and we all experienced the anguish of losing a father. And in that irrecoverable loss, I suspect none of us were able to hold back our mournful cries.

Up until now, as the head of a household, as a father, and as a human being, I had aspired to be Fujio Akatsuka's alter ego—Bakabon's dad. That won't be changing. At some point, when I wasn't looking, I aged past Bakabon's dad, who is forty-one. But even now, I remain unworthy of inheriting the name of "fool." To become a genius, I must already be a fool. To become a fool, I must become my naked self. And to be a fool, I must already be a genius. I don't want to surrender myself in the perpendicular space between fool and genius; I want to put myself on the same plane as them both. I want to believe that one day, after meditating on Bakabon's dad's sayings, "the opposition of agreement" and "the agreement of opposition," I will finally be able to reply to the greatest bit of nonsense Fujio Akatsuka devised.

In Bakabon's world, the sun rises in the west and sets in the east.

Is it correct? Is it wrong? Is it genius? Is it foolish? Or is it nonsense? It doesn't matter anymore.

It is my bare self, and the bare world in which Fujio Akatsuka lived.

"It'll be fine!"

■ FEBRUARY 2009

.

UNDER OUR WALKING SHELLS: THE LIBERATION OF MUSIC AND THE FUTURE SMARTPHONES WILL BRING

The Sony Walkman and the Apple iPod

Suppose someone says to you, "You are going to spend several weeks on an island." And then they say, "You can bring just one portable item with you."

What do you think today's youth would choose to bring? When people our age were still children, we probably would have agonized over the decision before finally choosing one well-used paperback.

In the 1970s, we couldn't walk around with music, movies, TV, or telephones. We had pocket-sized books and portable radios, but otherwise, any enjoyment of the aforementioned pastimes took place where all their respective devices accumulated—the family living room.

Then, in the last summer of the '70s, there came a revolutionary invention: Sony released a portable stereo cassette player, which they called a walking stereo—the Walkman TPS-L2. A little more than fifty years had passed since Iwanami Bunko brought paperback books to Japan. At last, mankind could carry music with them wherever they went; we became the walking man.

When the Walkman was first released, the news proclaimed it as a great achievement, but I wasn't all that impressed. I was a first-year senior high school student in a single-mother household. The price was beyond my reach; ignoring the gadget was my only real option. Then, one day two years later, in the spring, I was dozing off in class when my classmate's voice awoke me.

"Kojima, listen to this."

He handed me a small box connected to a pair of headphones, which I obediently put on. Then, I heard Akira Terao's singing voice, not as much through my ears as from inside my body. The song was "Habana Express," the first track of his album *Reflections*.

"Huh?!" I gasped.

I was speechless. The sound was three-dimensional. It was as if music had enveloped me. This wasn't like a home stereo system where the music flowed at me from a single direction. The sound was spilling out from inside me, almost soaking through into my vision. It felt like I was in the center of the sound.

"What is this?!" I finally managed to say.

That was when I learned that little box was a Walkman. But at the time, a personal music player was still a luxury beyond my reach. I couldn't think, "I want one right now!" The most I could hope for was, "I want one someday."

But then the following year, my circumstances changed completely. I began attending a university in another prefecture. Before that, I had always gone to school in my own school district and had walked there and back. But now going to school involved bus or train rides, with transfers, and each way took more than two hours. I needed to do something to combat the fatigue and stress of the terrible commute and to fill those vast stretches of time.

Armed with a proper justification to make the purchase, I triumphantly bought my very own Walkman in the spring of 1982. It was the WM-2, the second-generation Walkman, with the headphones padded with orange foam.

Like many other Walkman users, I was immediately enthralled by the magnificence of carrying music with me as I walked. Every mundane happening became a dramatic scene from a movie. The scenery from the train window, the once-familiar streets, the sunrises and sunsets, the darkness of night, the dense crowds of pedestrians in the city; with the real-time addition of music, everything looked different, as if transformed into something else. It was a strange sensation. This wasn't like the music I heard through speakers. Music spliced itself into the pathways of all five senses and amplified my emotions and memories. Sometimes I wept in the train station or on the street corner. Sometimes I skipped along the sidewalk or the stairs. The Walkman provided me my own personal soundtrack that made my days feel dramatic.

I kept on listening to my Walkman. I even used it at home. Whenever I did anything, I needed music that was mine and mine alone. Due to my Walkman dependence, I always overworked my players to the point that I felt sorry for them. On average, I junked a unit every two to three years. Each time, I replaced the Walkman with a new one. (I also cheated on Sony with Aiwa and Panasonic along the way.) Each new generation of Walkman returned with added features—the ability to record, to listen to FM radio, and an auto-reversing playback head. The evolution wasn't just functional; a variety of color options made the units more fashionable, much like has happened with the cell phones of today.

The headphones also made advancements. They became small enough to fit inside the listener's ears rather than resting over their head, and were equipped with remote control functions, and for a time, went wireless.

And the storage medium for the music was itself changing at a dizzying pace. In the mid-1980s came the Discman, which used CDs instead of cassette tapes, and in the '90s MiniDiscs took the place of CDs with the MD Walkman.

The Walkman holds a special place in my heart. The various incarnations of the portable music player supported me though half of my life. Whatever I was facing—through times of heartbreak, times of despair, times I made a mistake, times of sickness and ill health, times I was feeling low, times I was faced with loss, times I thought I would die, times I thought I might break under pressure, times I thought that stress was going to crush me, times I felt like I had failed at life, times my ideas had run dry—Walkman was there to prop me up. For half my life, Walkman and I walked together like two people with three legs between them.

Then, in October 2001, twenty-two years after the Walkman's debut, another new invention changed the world: Apple released the first-ever digital audio player, the iPod. Unlike previous analog media, music could now be downloaded directly to the internal hard drive inside the unit. Gone was the need for any physical media such as tapes or MiniDiscs. The leap from analog to digital access was revolutionary. In the blink of an eye, the iPod had taken over the world and even changed people's lifestyles. I was still an analog adherent, overworking my MD Walkman, but I joined the rest of the world four years later, when in 2005 I finally purchased an iPod mini 6 GB.

For Christmas in 2007, I gave my son his first iPod (the nano). I also impulse bought myself an iPod classic 120 GB. It is my third and current iPod (my second was the iPod 5.5).

The advent of the digital audio player enabled us to carry around more than just music. Various kinds of digital media could all be put into the same box (or pod). The iPod had been specifically designed to carry music, but it soon evolved into the iPod touch, and finally the iPhone, which is an all-purpose portable computer. I'm sure many users don't even put music on theirs.

Portable phones. Portable game consoles. Portable computers. Each began from a different starting point but are continually evolving and expanding their capabilities. Each is still categorized by separate names, but in the near future I have no doubt they will all converge and become able to do the exact same things. When that time comes, we'll all be able to take everything with us when we go out from our homes and our rooms—TV, radio, videos, pictures, music, the internet, our data, phones, and games. We'll be able to bring them along wherever in the world we go, even beyond national borders, and enjoy them at any time on our own terms, without anyone getting in the way. The walking man began with the liberation of music, and now through digitalization, has become a walking house—a pod—to carry all our various selves. But paradoxically, that also means we now have a movable shell—a pod—within which we can isolate ourselves from society any time or any place we wish.

I want you to think back to the hypothetical situation from the beginning of this essay. Someone tells you that you are to spend several weeks on an island. I don't think we need to bother discussing what people of today would choose to bring with them. But what if the question is replaced by an instruction: "You can take anything except your phone." How would people respond? I think most people of today would say, "If I can't use my phone, I'm not going." People can now carry around such a vast array of stuff; they've packed their phones with every kind of entertainment, their information, their lifestyles, and their individual consciousness. They carry everything on their person everywhere they walk. There is no active thought process deciding what one thing they need to take along. I think that because of that, they are forgetting the joy that was once found in portability. The selection was the real pleasure. Having abandoned the selection, they carry all of themselves inside a shell, which leads to greater isolation from society. The world had been maintaining a balance atop interpersonal confrontations.

If anything remains that has yet to be made portable, what will be the next thing we bring with us? Will adding anything else to our pockets enrich us any further? Will the added convenience bring us any happiness?

With such concerns in my thoughts, I nevertheless insert my earbuds and once again become, today as the days before, a man walking inside his own shell.

■ APRIL 2009

THE RETURN TO SPACE: THE RETURN FROM BEING A GAME DESIGNER

Space

> *I was only twelve and at school in the village of Gyuláháza in northeast Hungary when Gagarin flew. The peasants in the village were very down-to-earth people, and they greeted the news as something supernatural. Many were completely unwilling to believe that a man had been able to go so far from Earth.*
> —*Bertalan Farkas, Hungarian cosmonaut*

If I could have just one wish in my life—if I could cast a magic spell and make anything come true—without hesitation, it would be this: "I wish to go into space before I die." It doesn't have to be anything as extravagant as a trip to the moon or Mars. I would be satisfied with only a brief orbit, just beyond Earth's atmosphere, where I can gently brush against outer space. I would give up anything to make that wish come true: my current place as a game designer, which I've built up to for forty-five years; I'm even prepared to throw away my family or my own life. That is how powerfully I—or rather, *we*—yearn for the cosmos.

Why do I to this day still so admire astronauts? The answer is simple: because they are heroes above any other; they are the pioneers who challenge the unexplored realm with resolve and determination. The indomitable explorers face what no one has seen, endure rigorous training, and turn the unprecedented and impossible one by one into the possible. They are the chosen elite in rarefied possession of "the right stuff" (in body, mind, and spirit) necessary for their missions. *Astronaut* is not a profession, but an idealized form for those who dream, admired by all.

The Apollo 11 moon landing on July 20, 1969, left a greater impact on me than anything else. I still feel lucky to have been able to share in that moment as it happened. Watching the landing filled me with incomparable courage and hope for the future. On July 17, 1975, the Apollo–Soyuz docking left a strong impression of a different kind. It was the middle of the Cold War. We belonged to the West and were convinced that the Soviets, the leaders of the East, were to be feared. We were still operating under that mistaken impression when the spacecraft of the Americans and their fearsome rivals docked 20,000 kilometers over the Pacific Ocean, and inside those cramped spacecrafts, the crews from the hypothetical enemy nations shook hands in friendship. As I squinted at the blurry images on the television, I thought I was watching the moment that science changed human prejudices and ushered in a new era. That event moved me more deeply than watching the fall of the Berlin Wall.

My aspirations to become an astronaut naturally led me to become more and more of a science *otaku*. Every month, I used what little allowance I received on science magazines like *Newton* and *Omni* (the Japanese version). I watched documentary shows like Carl Sagan's *Cosmos* and *Shirarezaru Sekai* (The Unknown World). I never missed the frequent live broadcasts of space missions, which held higher priority than even my most beloved movies. Although I was hopeless at math, I was absolutely obsessed with science, and science magazines and TV shows excited me more than *Playboy* or the legendarily raunchy late-night talk show *11PM*. I tried to extend my reach by reading an extensive variety of Kodansha's Blue Back science books and science textbooks. I single-mindedly threw myself at biology, chemistry, geology, and other science classes. Everything was to bring me that much closer to becoming an astronaut and to prepare for the future when humanity went out to the stars.

Now I know why I'm here
Not for a closer look at the moon
But to look back
At our home
The Earth.

—Alfred Worden, American astronaut

But truthfully, I gave up on my dream of becoming an astronaut almost immediately upon entering senior high. Japan had a semigovernmental space development agency called NASDA, but even if I could make it in, they had no astronauts. (Later, a series of launch failures led to a consolidation of programs under a new Independent Administrative Institution by the name of JAXA, which had abandoned any plans on sending humans into space.) During the Cold War, crossing the Iron Curtain and becoming a cosmonaut in a country on the other side was preposterous. That left only one possible avenue: to join NASA in America. But not being an American, I wasn't going to have any chance of getting into NASA. It's not like I was going to change my citizenship. I had to give up. It sounds strange, but those simplistic excuses worked on a subconscious level to convince me to give up on my dreams and grow up. Be that as it may, I didn't give up on my dream to go into space; I only accepted that I would never be an astronaut as a profession. Even as a college student, hiding Takashi Tachibana's *Return from Space* in my pocket, I never forgot for a moment my yearning for outer space.

Then something big happened. A civilian—not a career astronaut—took another route into space. I don't hear people talk about it often, but the first Japanese citizen to go to space was not

JAXA's Mamoru Mohri; it was Toyohiro Akiyama, a correspondent for TBS (Tokyo Broadcasting System). On December 2, 1990, Akiyama launched aboard the Soyuz from the (then-Soviet) Baikonur Cosmodrome and became the first Japanese citizen to fly in space, and the first space correspondent.

"Ah! So that was another way!"

By then I was in the video game industry and had long since given up on any formal notion of becoming an astronaut. And now, with TBS's funding and Russia's technology, and without NASA's involvement at all, a civilian had gone to space. I stomped my feet in frustration for not seeing that pathway and simmered in total jealousy.

Then it hit me: I had never wanted to simply go into space. I wanted to go through the astronaut training program and go into space as an astronaut. What I had admired were the astronauts who made the impossible possible. And so, in 2008, when the first game designer went to space, I wasn't surprised either. I didn't feel the powerful envy like I did for Akiyama. The first game designer in space was Richard Garriott, world-class creator of *Ultima*. In October of last year (2008), he reportedly paid Russia $30 million and made the voyage from Baikonur Cosmodrome to the International Space Station.

"We went to the moon as technicians; we returned as humanitarians."
–Edgar Mitchell, American astronaut

The year 2009 is the International Year of Astronomy. Precisely four centuries have passed since Galileo Galilei first used a telescope to make astronomical observations, and four decades since Apollo 11 landed on the moon. Various events commemorating the occasion are being held in places all over the world, and space movies are coming out one after the other, including the Japanese premiere of the documentary *In the Shadow of the Moon* and BBC Worldwide's documentary *Rocketmen*. I hope that people who have been pushed away from space exploration will watch them. This might be hard to believe, but some young people today actually don't know that mankind has been going to the moon since before they were born. I particularly want them to see those movies. If they do, I think they'll come to understand why our generation idolized space and the astronauts. It's not that there's necessarily anything out there in space, but listening to the astronauts' stories and watching them face their challenges will doubtlessly inspire courage and dreams for the future. Anyone who sees them will feel pride at being a member of the same human race and will think, *Nothing is impossible for us!* And that's right, because forty years ago, humanity went to the moon and back.

Why do we want to go to the moon? Not to experience weightlessness. Not to meet extraterrestrial life. Not to be alone within the empty blackness. Not to feel the thrill of unmatched danger. Not for the pride of having a special experience. But to learn who we are and what our place is. To reexamine ourselves.

The journey to reach outer space is the journey to know oneself. To return from space is to return to Earth, and from the past self to the future self.

At some place, on a certain day, I liked space—looking back from outer space at our mother the planet Earth, what will I see there?

To where will I, a game designer, return?

"The first day or so we all pointed to our countries. The third or fourth day we were pointing to our continents. By the fifth day, we were aware of only one Earth."
—Sultan Bin Salman al-Saud, Saudi Arabian Astronaut

■ JUNE 2009

Quotations are from The Home Planet, *edited by Kevin W. Kelley for the* Association of Space Explorers.

AFTERWORD

From Memes to Strands

In June of 2016 in Los Angeles, during a press conference at E3, the world's largest video game trade show, I presented the first reveal trailer for *Death Stranding*. Half a year had passed since I founded Kojima Productions as an independent studio on December 16.

My thoughts were filled with all the many things that had happened since my last E3 two years earlier.

The two-year gap seemed like decades.

On the stage, I announced, "I'm back," and the members of the press who had gathered in the auditorium and people watching the streaming video all over the world met me with a warm welcome. That was the moment I knew that my decision to go independent and to continue making video games had not been the wrong one.

While I was still searching for staff and technology and physical space for my new studio, I went to meet with Norman Reedus, offered him the leading role in *Death Stranding*, and then made the first trailer over the span of about two and a half months. Our studio moved into our current office three weeks before E3.

When I said that we would be able to put together the announcement entirely on our own under those conditions, people didn't want to believe me.

This might sound paradoxical, but we were only able to do it *because* we didn't outsource or have a clear division of labor.

In the name of better efficiency, outsourcing and division of labor have become standard not just in big-budget Hollywood movie productions but the video game industry as well. But I can't categorically agree with that approach.

What makes me say that is my now-ingrained, unwavering style, from which I use my own eyes and head and body to discern artistic quality and find the one-in-ten "winners."

I often take walks through my studio, just as I do in my daily bookstore visits. (This is still true in our current setup, although we all share one floor now and are close enough to see each other.) I find solutions for the problems of the hour right where they occur, then give the appropriate direction. I'm convinced that our ability to make high-quality work in a short period of time is because the teams are small enough to allow for that level of involvement.

Just as I can't stand in front of a bookstore and input "new release novel winner," and press SEARCH, I can't run a search query in the studio to find the right solutions. The answers only exist inside myself. For that purpose, I have to keep honing my eye and my sensibilities.

In the original edition of this book, I wrote:

> *The world is connected with ME + ME.*
> *Memes are propagated when people connect with each other. Stories dwell inside everyone and everything, no matter who or what they are. The act of reading stories, telling them, and sharing them with others is the way that ME + ME connect across time and place.*

Stories dwell inside everyone and everything, no matter who or what they are. And the meanings of those stories will change based on the time and circumstances in which they are read. Then, left to each individual recipient, certain elements will be imitated, and others expanded. Through that repeated behavior, new memes are born.

In that moment, multiple fragmented copies of "me" become one.

Typically, it happens when elements not directly within your attention suddenly connect. This may seem like happenstance, but I understand the meeting to be inevitable and prearranged.

I don't mean that in the sense of some occult influence or divine possession. By proactively seeking out and taking in memes, we bring them to us and enable their connections. I believe that is the foundation of creating new memes.

To give an example, the E3 reveal trailer used a song by a band called Low Roar, and I came across their music in much the same way.

Before *Death Stranding* existed in any shape or form, I went to Iceland on vacation. While I was there, I got into a taxi, and the driver turned out to be a member of a band called kimono, who are known as the Icelandic Joy Division. He recommended a CD store to me, so I went, picked out a few CDs, and went to buy them at the register. Just then, I heard a song playing on the store's sound system, and I liked it and asked who it was. It was Low Roar. I bought their album too and went back to Japan.

At this point, that music was just "with" me. I'd found it, and it was fermenting at the bottom of my awareness, but it hadn't yet been born into a new meme.

Then, when I was in the trial-and-error process of figuring out what to do for the trailer's music, I suddenly thought of Low Roar's "I'll Keep Coming."

ME + ME connected as if the union had been planned from the start, and a new meme came to life.

Because this trailer was to be the very first announcement of a completely new property, from a marketing standpoint, I maybe should've used a more well-known song. But to do it that way would've been no different from sitting at my desk and googling "new hit songs." I would only find ideas that already existed.

This approach wasn't limited to the music, either. The cast of actors for *Death Stranding* came about the same way, starting with Norman Reedus and Mads Mikkelsen. I had seen them acting and liked them. Because I liked them, I wanted to meet them. I thought I'd like to work with them one day. Following that course, I met with them in real life. The moment I did, I knew immediately that we would work well together. The same thing happened with directors Guillermo del Toro and Nicolas Winding Refn, who did their cameos as personal favors. Refn was even nice enough to say that meeting me was like "reuniting with a childhood friend."

It's probably safe to say this process only works because of my perceptivity for "hits," which I honed in bookstores, and the conviction that connections are what we make.

When it comes to making a product that will sell and be accepted by the world at large, I won't deny the viability of a marketing-oriented approach that examines past successes and uses the elements that made them sell. But I don't want to do things that way. It's not interesting.

If today were to last forever, a marketing-oriented process based on past data might be fine. But tomorrow will always come. The things of the past will not go on being accepted unchanged. Yesterday's experiences are not all that exists. You cannot assume that if yesterday was a certain way, today will be the same.

That said, past experiences are necessary to create new connections. That's why I read books, watch movies, and listen to music. I go to art and history museums. I meet people.

That repeated process is the only way to learn from history and create the future.

The future cannot be created through simple imitation of the memes other people made in the past—even if from the business standpoint, that might be a safe, low risk method.

ME + ME has a plus in the middle—I believe that act of connection is a critical component. People like people who have something they do not. That's true in love, but it's also the foundation that builds friendships. Creative works are like that too. Just like continuously interbreeding similar genetic material will diminish variety and lead to an evolutionary dead end, memes will not evolve and progress without the introduction of new connections.

A person can only meet so many people within the span of their lives. The same applies to memes, to say nothing of drawing the one-in-ten winners. But through books, movies, and music, we can meet vastly more people and have vastly more experiences than is possible in real life.

Our inherited genes alone do not make a person complete. By adding up a variety of experiences and absorbing memes, as through books, we grow as individuals.

When I was still a student who hadn't come into his own, and wasn't yet a video game designer, I was able to keep going thanks to the memes told through stories. Whenever I was worried or uncertain about my future, I looked to stories for my compass. By experiencing unfamiliar times and places, I expanded my own world and was able to refine my outlook and perceptivity.

Eventually, I became able to make a living through artistic creation, and my approach toward my relationship with stories began to shift. The way I connected with them, the way I connected them together, the way I used the plus in ME + ME, and the nature of that "plus" changed. I began to think not just within my own bubble, but about how I could connect with my players and the world through the memes of my works. I want to make people take another step forward; to give a push on the backs of the people who are standing in place. I want to make the world better. And so, my thoughts have turned completely to how I could connect "me" and "me" to make that happen, and how I would form new memes.

Sometimes, as I continue my creative work, I will be hounded by intense feelings of isolation, or troubled by stress and doubt. In times like those, I am saved by the existence of other people whose mentality is similar to mine. This of course includes creative figures like writers, directors, and artists, but could be anyone who tries to connect "me" and "me" to make new memes. Their struggles save me from my loneliness. Their struggles are themselves another story and another meme.

Say that someone in some faraway country made an incredible creative work, and that it was a big hit. Through watching it, or reading it, or however the work is experienced, I am able to believe that I can still keep trying. They push me onward.

If you lived in a time when no one had ever been to the moon, and you said, "I am going to the moon," others might flatly dismiss you and respond, "Come on, people could never go there." But what if someone in a faraway country did just that, and in that country, they became heroes? You would know that it *was* possible to go to the moon after all. All those people who scorned your dream would no longer matter a damn to you, and you would feel emboldened to try for yourself.

Moreover, people have created stories about going to the moon for a very long time, and those stories connected through the culture. The stories became reality for that reason. Stories and fiction are often criticized as escapism. But in fiction is truth. Fiction can also be a tool at the forefront of the fight to correct the problems of reality.

I believe in the power of stories and memes. They enrich us and the world at large. And so I want to tell my stories and pass them on. I want to tell a great many stories, and to build connections between people and each other, and across worlds and times. Those connections may become "the creative genes" that will present us with worlds no one has ever experienced before.

The Creative Gene will form connections—strands—between me and you, and maybe new memes will be made.

Toward that hope, I will once again visit a bookstore today and search for strands that I have not yet seen.

■ **HIDEO KOJIMA, JULY 2019**

WHAT ARE CONNECTIONS?

A Conversation with Gen Hoshino and Hideo Kojima

GEN HOSHINO was born in Saitama Prefecture in 1981, and is a musician, actor, and writer. His first solo album, *Baka no Uta*, was released in 2010. His October 2016 single "Koi" became a cultural phenomenon as the title song to *The Full-Time Wife Escapist*, a TV drama in which he also played the leading role. In December 2018, he released his fifth album, *Pop Virus*. In August 2019, he performed for 330,000 people across Japan's five major sports domes and released a live-concert video, *Dome Tour Pop Virus at Tokyo Dome*. His writings include *Soshite Seikatsu Wa Tsuzuku*, *Hataraku Otoko*, *Hoshino Gen Zatsudanshu 1*, *Inochi no Shaso Kara*, and *Yomigaeru Hentai*. He also starred in the August 2019 film *Samurai Shifters*.

HIDEO KOJIMA: How long would you say we've known each other?

GEN HOSHINO: You let me interview you in 2012 for my article series *Hoshino Gen no 12-nin no Osoroshii Nihonjin* (Gen Hoshino's 12 formidable Japanese people) in *POPEYE* magazine (collected in Magazine House's *Hoshino Gen Zatsudanshu 1*).

KOJIMA: So that makes it seven years then.

HOSHINO: Seven years! Yeah, I guess so.... Before you offered to talk with me today, I happened to watch some cutscenes from the *Metal Gear Solid* series at home.

There's a scene in *Metal Gear Solid 4: Guns of the Patriots* where Big Boss kneels in front of The Boss's grave and thinks back to how she told him, "Respect the will of others and believe in your own." That game was released in 2008, so you probably thought of that line sometime earlier than that. That would be before social media became so widespread. But I think those words express a sentiment we now need more than any other. Respecting the thoughts of others will lead to respecting your own. Accepting someone else's existence will lead to accepting your own. But we're all not doing very well at that. When I first played through that game, that line moved me. But watching that scene again, I realized that you recognized that sentiment more than ten years ago and worked it into your story. I think very few creators are able to incorporate messages into their works with the same level of sophistication as you. That's what I really like about you.

That, and—I'm sure you hear this all the time, but I also love the kind of humor that only you can express—having the player set the controller down and having it vibrate on its own, that kind of thing. I mean, how can you not laugh at that?

KOJIMA: You know, sometimes I surprise myself.

HOSHINO: You have a knack for taking some really specific detail, something that would make everyone at the team meeting or whatever laugh and talk about how it's funny, and that would be the end of it...but then you have the conviction to put it into the game, and let us in on the joke. I'm always trying to think of ideas, whether it's for music or some other kind of personal expression, but I'm just part of a team, and the team has to make it reality. Whenever I come across your humor in your games, I'm always reminded that if I'm going to make an interesting idea into reality, I can never give up on it.

KOJIMA: And to always be thinking of ideas, you have to live with your receptive antennae always out and scanning in all directions around you. That's incredibly draining. But when you're always exposing yourself to all the diverse things around you, taking the parts that catch at your interest and turning them around and around in your mind, and then bringing that into form and putting it out into the world—that's how things are created. A person who can do that can do anything. In Japan, we treat people who have achieved mastery at something as only capable of doing that one thing, but that's of course not true.

Take yourself—you're doing music and acting. You're also really good at writing essays, which pisses me off, actually. [*laughs*] But you can do that because you go through life always soaking in a variety of things and thinking about them like that. If they come back out in words, that's an essay. If it's lyrics or sound, that's music. Or they could come through your technique as an actor.

In the same way, I've kept my antennae open to stimuli all around me as I've made video games for more than thirty years, and I don't feel that the process of creating games itself is hard anymore. Even though in November *Death Stranding* is going to be released after three and a half years in development.

HOSHINO: Three and a half years.... That's pretty short, isn't it?

KOJIMA: This time around, I had to put together a new company; that part was harder than making the game. When I went independent, I had to find people who would make games with me and a place to make them in. When you quit a company, you don't have any credibility, and even getting a loan to start a company takes great effort. Thankfully, all the fans of my earlier games helped me in ways I hadn't anticipated. I managed to cast Hollywood actors in *Stranding* because I had been able to meet actors who liked *Metal Gear* and who wanted to do a role because they wanted to do it. Since we shared a mutual affinity, I was lucky enough to meet them directly, in person.

HOSHINO: Right. If someone else gets in the middle, it can be hard to communicate what you want to say, even though a one-on-one conversation should have worked—as if different aspects of the situation can get in the way and weaken what you're trying to say.

This might be an impertinent thing to say to someone of your stature, but I feel like I sympathize with what you're trying to do. It's like the things that you want to do naturally bring about something new to the world.

KOJIMA: I never run out of things I want to do, because technology is always advancing. Ideas come to me with absolutely no effort, although sometimes my team will have things to say about them. They're supposed to be on my side, but sometimes I'm making something because I believe in my heart it will be interesting, and they'll say, "No one has ever done that before. It'll never work," or, "What part of that is interesting?" or, "You can't do that," and they'll put on the brakes. But almost nothing is impossible.

Project Apollo succeeded fifty years ago. Three astronauts went all the way to the surface of the moon, where no one had ever gone before, and they came back. When you hear that, don't you feel like you could do anything?

Conversely, if you yourself think something isn't turning out to be interesting, you should absolutely stop right there. I'm sure that happens when you're writing songs, right?

HOSHINO: It does. I could be 80 percent finished with a song when I realize, I should stop here—even if I finished it 100 percent, this one won't be exciting.

KOJIMA: With video games, you don't truly know if it's going to be fun until you actually play it. And when you do play your game, and it's not fun, it's extremely important to be able to perceive if that's because your idea was implemented and your idea isn't fun, or if the game isn't fun because your idea isn't coming through.

When I was making *Metal Gear*, I started with the idea of a game where the player hides and escapes from enemies, and I made the concept into a game and played it. At that point, if it's not fun, what should be the next step? To investigate whether the concept of hiding and escaping from enemies isn't properly there in the game yet, or if the concept of hiding and escaping from enemies itself just isn't fun. If it's the latter, then I should stop making that game then and there. If I start doing what marketing or whoever tells me to do,

I'll lose the ability to make that decision to turn back, and the end result would be a typical video game like any other.

HOSHINO: In our first conversation, you told me that if someone wanted to create something, they'd better become a producer. I'm also my own producer, so people rarely tell me, "That's bad," or "No, *you* do it." But on the flip side, I have to think about everything and make the decisions myself. It feels like I'm always fighting with myself, you know?

With *Doraemon the Movie: Nobita's Treasure Island*, I was put in charge of doing the opening song, and I wanted to call it "Doraemon." You just don't see anime songs that use the same title as the anime anymore. But I thought it was a fun idea, and I proposed it. As expected, the corporate side said, "No, we don't think that would work." There was a problem with the trademark or something, and wouldn't it be troublesome to use the title of such a tremendously huge property, they said. But especially because everyone else has stopped naming songs after anime, I thought there would be meaning in facing such a universally known title as *Doraemon* head-on. My role was to write a song that would be used in the anime as a cross-promotion—but the more radical idea would be to write the song directly *for* the anime. So I pushed back and said, "Please, just ask if it's possible or not."

Of course, I had to be coming from a place of respect toward the property. I had to show sincerity, and I had to communicate that I was passionate about the project to warrant going to Fujiko Productions and Shin-Ei Animation for permission. But as I started doing that work, the team's mood began to change from, "If you do that, they'll be mad at us, and we're scared," to, "It would be cool if you pulled it off." I've been able to keep going because I know from previous experiences that the people around me will get excited in the end.

KOJIMA: I think you could absolutely make a video game.

HOSHINO: No way! [*laughs*] But I think *you* could probably make music.

KOJIMA: I basically want to do *everything* myself, and I really would like to make music, but I just can't get anything to come out. Sometimes I'll think I have an idea, and I'll sing it to myself and think, "Hey, I think I've made something," but then it turns out to be another song I've heard, and I feel disappointed.

HOSHINO: I don't know, I feel like you just haven't gotten off to a start yet. I think if you break through your limits and just put something out there, even if you have to force it, you'll get off the ground. I understand wanting to put out something really good because you're passionate about it, but if you put out something—even if it isn't pretty—I think that since this is you, it would be real music.

KOJIMA: That's a good point. Putting something out into the world might be an important part. *Death Stranding* is an especially new kind of game, and I worry about whether it will be accepted or not. Playing the game is kind of like climbing Mt. Fuji by yourself. It can be a hard time. You might stop partway and think, "Why am I putting myself through this much trouble?" and give up. But when you climb all the way to the summit and see the rising sun, and all the effort and hardship will be validated, you'll probably start to cry. That's the kind of game it is. But you can't cry if you turn back without going all the way to the summit.

HOSHINO: I wonder like that will be like.... You've said that "connections" are a theme.

KOJIMA: This is a little bit of a spoiler, but the main character, Sam Bridges, can come across a man who will die without his regular delivery of medicine. Sam is a deliverer and is asked to bring him the medicine. And by doing so, he forms a connection with the man.

But the man has no direct bearing on the story's plot, and depending on the player, they may forget to bring him the medicine. And if they stop bringing the medicine, the man will die.

HOSHINO: Really? Whoa, you've put in quite the heartrending gimmick, haven't you?

KOJIMA: To build a connection with another person is also to take on responsibility toward them. I want the players to experience that their actions can make connections as well as break them.

HOSHINO: I think that what makes your games so dangerous is that they make the player think not just through the game's dialogue and storylines, but by the actions the player takes inside the game. Like the scene in *Metal Gear Solid 3: Snake Eater*, where you force the player to choose to kill or not kill The Boss. I still remember that like it was yesterday.

KOJIMA: I want the players to experience things that are only possible within video games and that have never been done before. Otherwise, there's no point in making the game.

In *Stranding*, players can't meet other players in the same way as in an open-world online game, but they can leave things behind for others who pass through the same place, and the other players can respond back by leaving "likes."

Say for example that you are playing the game, and you're walking along a path and decide to leave a device that plays a song there. Later on, some other person will be walking along the same path and start to hear music. They'll wonder why someone else left that device there. All they can really infer from what you left is that maybe you liked that music. But they'll feel connected to someone else. They thought they had been walking in solitude but are made to see that they aren't alone.

It's easy now to connect with people on social media, but our relationships are becoming ones where we just talk directly at each other, right? I see some people who communicate using absolutely no imagination toward the people to whom they're talking. With *Stranding*, I want to show a different kind of connection—a cushioned connection. I wanted to make a story where the player has to use their imagination to figure out who else is there and what they are thinking.

HOSHINO: By making the connections indirect, the player can more strongly feel other people's presence and minds. Like the mother in Kazuo Umezz's *The Drifting Classroom*. [*laughs*] I can't wait to play it.

I should also thank you for putting a place inside the game where the players can listen to one of my songs.

KOJIMA: I did. Players can listen to your song in a place called the "private room." I do hope you will play the game and try it out. Without my connection with you, I wouldn't have been able to include your music. I believe that creating things is only possible through connections with other people, and works, and history, and all kinds of other things. Then, that newly created work will give someone else a push and move the world forward. I want to keep on doing that as long as I live.

■ AUGUST 2019

ABOUT THE AUTHOR

Born in Tokyo in 1963, **HIDEO KOJIMA** is a world-renowned video game creator, and a well-known movie and novel aficionado. He made his directorial debut in 1987 with *Metal Gear*, which became a series and provided the foundation for the stealth game genre. In 2001, he was selected as one of the ten most influential people in *Newsweek* magazine's special feature "Who's Next." At the end of 2015, Kojima established Kojima Productions, his own independent studio. He has received international recognition, entering the Hall of Fame at the 2016 DICE Awards and receiving the Industry Icon Award at The Game Awards in 2016. In 2019, Kojima released his long-awaited new game *Death Stranding*.

ABOUT THE TRANSLATOR

NATHAN A COLLINS studied Japanese at the University of Iowa and the Yamasa Institute in Okazaki and has been a translator of novels, manga, and video games for more than a decade. His credits include *Battle Royale*, *Metal Gear Solid: Guns of the Patriots*, and *JoJo's Bizarre Adventure*, as well as entries in the *Tales of* and *Rune Factory* series. He's a gamer dad who bought his PlayStation to play *Metal Gear Solid* and says: keep on keeping on.

CREDITS

MEDIA LIST

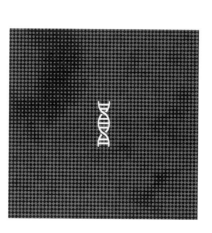